The poetic embrace like the carnal

While it endures

Forbids all lapse into the miseries of the world

—*André Breton*

SURREALISM:

the road to the absolute

anna balakian

the noonday press

new york

to Stepan and to Nona

foreword

◐

Since the time of Baudelaire, poetry in France has been gradually severing its connections with the rest of literature. It linked its fate with art, and the two together began to encroach on the domain of philosophy. The poetic image, completely revolutionized, ceased to be considered as merely a source of aesthetic pleasure and became a new instrument of metaphysical knowledge for the poet. The persistent searchings into self and the universe broadened the scope of human imagination. Poetic vision came to be linked with the credo of existence in modern society's dilemma between surrender to the existing limits of the human condition and man's stubborn longing for spiritual release from them. For four generations of poets, writing became the barometer for the delicate changes they discerned in the moral and philosophical atmosphere in which they lived. This study will attempt to trace the road upon which they marked their progress.

The present study is a continuation of my earlier book, *Literary Origins of Surrealism,* which I wrote in my twenties. In the years that have elapsed since then, I never ceased to explore the rich vein of modern French poetry, and I am not hesitant today to consider the surrealists and their antecedents as a liberating force against the neo-nineteenth-century aspects of much of the literature of our time. Some parts of this study have appeared in abbreviated form in scholarly journals in the course of the past ten years, namely the chapter on Apollinaire and part of the chapter on Aragon and Eluard in *Yale French Studies,* while a shorter version of "The Surrealist Image" was published in *The Romantic Review.* I wish to thank these periodicals for permission to reprint.

In the course of my investigations I have been to France, and I have met some of the poets and artists about whom I have been writing, but the reading and writing took place in the U.S., away from the physical surroundings of literary France; I have tried to judge by the testimony of the written word and have made an effort to disregard biographical events or the psychological and political conflicts of the moment. I would like to believe that geographical distance may have helped me to avoid some of the pitfalls connected with literary criticism when the time perspective is missing.

The prose and poetry translations from the French writers whom I have quoted are all mine. If they should cast a burlap screen over the original, may they spur those of my readers who do not understand French to make an effort to liberate themselves from the necessity of "secondhand" reading of the exciting and dynamic literature that France unceasingly produces in our day!

I shall never forget the kindness and sympathy that Pierre Reverdy and André Breton demonstrated in the enlightening, revealing conversations which I had with each of them. I am deeply thankful to my understanding husband for the encouragement which he has given me in my work. I am ever grateful for the sound judgment, wise counsel, and sharp editorial eye of my critic-sister, Nona. Finally, I feel very fortunate to have as my editor, Cecil Hemley, a poet himself, who believes that the discussion of poetry is a timely thing and that the mysticism of the poet, modified to the needs of our day, is a significant aspect of the literary scene.

New York, June 1959

the signal lights

ONE
Out of the Forest of Symbols : 3

TWO
Lautréamont's Battle with God : 20

THREE
Saint-Pol-Roux and the Apocalypse : 39

FOUR
Apollinaire and the Modern Mind : 50

FIVE
*Pierre Reverdy and the Materio-mysticism
of Our Age : 70*

the road

SIX
*Breton and the Surrealist Mind—The Influences
of Freud and Hegel : 91*

SEVEN
The Surrealist Image : 112

EIGHT
The Surrealist Object : 142

the bend in the road

NINE
The Post-Surrealism of Aragon and Eluard : 165

TEN
To Transform the World : 188

ELEVEN
The World Transformed : 197

EPILOGUE : 203

INDEX : 207

the signal lights

◑

out of the forest of symbols

The multifarious ramifications of the literary expression called "symbolism" have served as a *trompe l'oeil* for almost a century. In France it was the name of the literary coterie which between 1885 and 1895 rallied the poetic incertitudes into a concerted theory of indecision, and in England, Germany and America, it has been identified for a much more prolonged time with the extreme subjectivity of writers who cultivated mystification with the elusive-

ness of indirect discourse, and who in the process of refin-
ing their senses lost them in a whirlpool of synaesthesia.
The sustained introspection led to a desolate subtraction
of self from the integrated universe. Symbolism, originally
intended as a countermovement to naturalism, actually
turned out to be a variation of it rather than its antithesis.
If the Naturalist presumed the human will to be enslaved
to the physical forces of nature, the symbolist of those
end-of-the-century years was not far behind in acquiescing
in somewhat equivocal statements to the fatality of non-
subjective forces. If in the Naturalist's eye man is a product of chemistry, the symbolist's world of ineffable forces
is just as totally, though somewhat more somberly, controlled. For the symbolists, the forest of symbols, casually
mentioned by Baudelaire in a little sonnet to which he
himself attributed very little importance, is an inescapable labyrinth from which man cannot liberate his imagination; this is much the same situation in which the Nat-
uralists place the human personality when they judge it
powerless to overcome its physical and social limitations.
Both points of view reveal man's destiny as controlled by
forces other than his will, and the most formidable of
these elements is death, whether it be considered as something determined and tangible, or as an incomprehensible
intruder intertwining itself between the light and the wind.
Both concur in accepting the helplessness of man's condition on earth, and it is this basic similarity which made it
logical for a J. K. Huysmans or a Gerhardt Hauptmann
to proceed from one movement to the other.

The flight from consciousness into the dream-mystique,

he French Symbolists, was in a
Rimbaud's farewell to literature
light from writing into a life of
contemplative self. Indeed, what
evident as we progress into the
ieth century is that there was no
poraneous to naturalism, to hold
creasing fatalism and the depres-
over the arts. Only individual in-
ply moments in an individual's
as of a latent rebellion against the
festering tendencies of both naturalism and its would-be
antithesis, symbolism.

Indubitably the influence of these two literary movements has been tremendous in the twentieth century. The
tone of pessimism they encouraged in Western literature
bore the mark of nineteenth-century literary and philosophical concepts, regardless of the modifications made by
succeeding generations.

Although in their early years the surrealists revered
the symbolists as their spiritual elders, their approach to
art and the human condition was radically different. They
noted that although the literary techniques of symbolism were being maintained by a majority of their contemporaries, the fame of the nineteenth-century French
Symbolists was proving very precarious. André Breton observed in 1936 how the members of the Mallarmé school
sank one after the other into the sands of oblivion.[1] The
surrealists did not seek their heritage in literary movements of the past but in certain individual writers associ-

ated with that past: isolated intuitions which served as signal flares to clarify their own fresh vision of the arts.

William Blake was one of the earliest of these spiritual forebears, but not the Blake who expressed himself through Christian symbols. Rather, the surrealists have seen Blake as a visionary in Rimbaud's sense of the term and have extolled him for rejecting exterior reality as a subject of artistic expression and for transforming the physical world in his effort to alter its dimensions. Blake's eye, they thought, absorbed but did not determine: as an intermediary instrument, a recorder of physical sensation, it left the matter of interpreting to the imaginative faculty. By refusing to make of nature the object of aesthetic creation, Blake had removed painting and verbal imagery from the controlling factors of phenomenal reality. Blake has been admired by the surrealists because like them he made of poetry a way of life:[2] his pictorial and poetic imagery was the overflow of a spiritual crisis and his art asserted man's creative capacities.

In France, the poets with whom the surrealists and their sympathizers found most empathy were three who are very often associated with the word "symbolist," particularly in Anglo-Saxon literary criticism: Baudelaire, Lautréamont, and Rimbaud. In the case of Baudelaire, it was not the poem, "Correspondances" which attracted their interest, but the haunting presence of "the abyss" in certain of his works, its stimulation of the poetic imagination. Whereas the Romanticists, contemporary with Baudelaire, had been stretching their visions outward and upward, Baudelaire had projected his vistas downward

and inward, not in exaltation but with hesitancy and ap-
prehension. His cosmos is not far, but just beyond his
window and in the vertiginous fringe between sleep and
the dream, the pit of the subconscious where desire and
deed are undistinguishable, where time and space have
relationships other than those of the outer world. This
sensation of prodigious physical and spiritual depth which
obsessed Baudelaire at times, became the basis of a mysticism discovered in Baudelaire and developed as a credo
and technique in much of contemporary French poetry.
But what has elevated Baudelaire so far above the symbolists in the esteem of modern poets is the tension of his
life experience which matched the pitch of the poetry.
Whereas his fellow-symbolists were to efface their lives before their art and satisfy their mysticism with a lulling of
the senses, for Baudelaire writing was intensified living.
He never lost the sense of life and even his exploration of
artificial paradises was a desire for keener perceptivity:
"It is in effect, at this period of the rapture that a new
keenness, a superior acuity of all the senses is manifested.
The sense of smell, sight, hearing, touch participate
equally in this progression. The eyes aim at the infinite.
The ear perceives undiscernible sounds in the midst of
the vast tumult. This is when the hallucinations begin.
Exterior objects assume slowly, successively, singular appearances. They are deformed and transformed." [3]

Baudelaire had many more reasons than Villiers' *Axel*
to join his ancestors, but he chose life and the uncom-
promised will of the artist. He did not move through
a forest of symbols but on the contrary constantly sought

the concrete as the substance of his poetic alchemy. Axel expected nothing from life; Baudelaire expected much, too much to be ever requited, but also he sought for it too persistently ever to concede defeat.

Lautréamont, who died before he actually lived a normal life span, is another example of an energetic coming to grips with life; and it is hard to see how by any stretch of terminology he can be grouped among the symbolists.[4] He was an utter realist who in his most extreme cries of bitter combat against human destiny did not lose sight of the object of his strife: the world. Escape into death or into the dream is for him a puerile approach to the human condition. Lautréamont acknowledges the tragic character of life but the vigor of his struggle belies any real pessimism. It is this very distinction between recognizing the tragic and surrendering to it that proves to be the crux of the philosophical difference between symbolism and surrealism.

In claiming adherence to Rimbaud, the surrealists did not mean the Rimbaud who talked of himself but the one who said "*I* is another," not the one who burned in his private hell or who dropped the struggle with imagination to yield to the superficial escape of voyage. It is rather the poet who at moments had the most optimistic literary outlook of the last half of the nineteenth century, saying that man can reach seer-like knowledge: the poet who called himself an inventor, who sang of new flowers, new love, and who intimated the upsurging of unheard-of harmonies and visions, insisting that the whole world was in need of transformation. What misled many into associating Rimbaud with the symbolists was his personal relationship with one symbolist, Verlaine. But, whereas Verlaine sought pale, melted blues, misty skies, indistinct snows as landscapes for his "grey song," and in his *Art poétique* made a slogan of: "no color, nothing but the nuance," his fellow-traveler, Rimbaud, was proving a companion only in the actual voyage and not in the spiritual journey of literary experience.

Rimbaud saw not monotonous wastelands, but green hills and slopes, invigorating streams, indigos, and wished to possess all possible landscapes in his constant apostrophes to the "world." He strove to match the "fecundity of the mind" with the "immensity of the universe" by endeavoring to free the mind from its long bondage as prisoner of reason. Rimbaud's use of language, is not at all linked with the Symbolists' cult of indirect or veiled meaning. If Rimbaud's visions are sometimes incomprehensible, it is because they are too specific rather than too vague. He differs sharply from the Symbolists in the substantial, concrete character of his imagery which twentieth century French poets found worthier of imitation than the rare, pure vocabulary of the Symbolists.[5]

In an early moment of his career, Mallarmé, not yet lost in a search for pure abstractions, produced a work unlike anything he wrote later, called *Igitur,* in which he conveyed his preoccupations with the occult forces of physical life and his attempt to discover the inherent mystical qualities of material existence. This was a far cry from his friend Villiers' imitation of the same process in *Axel.* Whereas Axel's journey to the tomb was a desire

to escape from life and its imperfections in a sort of nihil-
istic comprehension of freedom, Igitur's exploration of
the process of death is an affirmation of the strength of
the mind to experience here and now the infinite or nothingness. Here, the concept of eternity is not envisaged as
something beyond the grasp of the senses, or to be com-
prehended only through symbols or abstractions. Instead
of speculating about immortality after death like Ham-
let, he seeks the absolute which *denies* immortality. But
this absolute which is subservient neither to life nor death,
is not a spiritualization of reality, as much of symbolist
poetry was to become; nor is it a denuding of the earthly
scene: the void or vacuum of symbolist landscapes. Nor
does it constitute a verbalization of the abstract, as in
Victor Hugo's metaphysical verse, or in the more recent,
more familiar T. S. Eliot end of the world, such as:

Between the desire
And the spasm
Between the potency
And the existence
Between the essence
And the descent
Falls the Shadow

   The Hollow Men

Unlike most symbolist imagery, the death vision in Mallarmé's *Igitur* is represented in terms of known and very
concrete entities of the world, though they be somewhat
divested of external trappings. But if the absolute is not
understood as the subjective perpetuation of perfected hu-

man experience after death, how will the poet convey "the substance of nothingness"? The very contradiction in terms gives the key to the answer. The existence of the absolute can be established only through the acceptance of the absurd, illustrated with an image such as of "panels opened and closed at the same time." For the difference between the finite world and the infinite is that in the former we recognize the juxtaposition of opposites as "absurd," while the power of "chance" which nullifies this contradiction in things can be said, from our point of view, "to contain the absurd." But the very fact that contradictions are reconciled by the forces of "chance" makes Igitur believe that the absurd no longer exists. The infinite, therefore, is the plane of reality in which combinations that we might call absurd in the normal order of things or logically impossible are accepted as possible. And this "chance" which turns what we call "absurd" into reality, permits, by that same token, the infinite to exist: he sees inanimate objects losing their natural attributes without being dissolved into abstractions. Sound is reduced to the beat, rhythm divested of sound, breaking down the barrier between the visual and the auditory.

"Briefly, in an act in which hazard is involved, it is always hazard which accomplishes its own Idea by self-affirmation or self-denial. Before its existence negation and affirmation come to failure. It contains the Absurd—implies it, but in a latent state and prevents it from existing: this permits the Infinite to exist." Igitur is a person "who feels in himself, thanks to the absurd, the existence of the Absolute." After him the surrealists will enlarge

and maintain the domain of the absolute through this very
same type of cult of the absurd which will tend to become the basis of artistic creation and a means of liberating art from the finite or natural aspects of things and
beings.[6]

Except for isolated cases such as mentioned above, there
was no concerted spiritual combat against the nihilism
dominating the minds and activities of the artists of the
end of the century. There was a weary acceptance of de-
cadence, of a hot-house atmosphere in which the vague
and the lifeless were synonymous with mystery, and the
mysterious was confused with the profound. In the best
of Symbolist works this sadness created a kind of exqui-
site, ephemeral beauty, as perhaps best embodied in Maeterlinck's character of fragile Mélisande, who does not know
what she is, where she comes from or where she is going,
but accepts this unreal existence, only to be swallowed up
by death at the end. But eventually the repetitious use of
the same type of weightless, shadowy imagery, populat-
ing a shut-in world, created an inverted kind of poetry,
exhausted the already limited word-range of pure, abstract expression and made French literature ready not
only for a new outlook but for an actual revolution in literary vocabulary and imagery.

The reaction is first sensed in the much neglected, so-
called symbolist poet, Saint-Pol-Roux; it is much more evident in the vigorous poetry of Apollinaire who envisioned
the poet not submerged in the vaporous hinterlands of
the symbolists, but in a state of ascent above his brethren.
Apollinaire came to grips with the object instead of con-

sidering it an obstacle to self-edification. As he viewed the things man has invented, he felt optimism and predicted the space age along with its challenge to the human imagination. He rejected the passiveness and torpor of his elders, extricating himself from the forest of symbols so that he might survey the wide expanses from the summit of his hill, and speculate on "what life really is." Then man would wake to new knowledge. His whole poem is a reaffirmation of faith in the human potential to master the universe. Even the war, in which he participated actively and in which he received a wound which eventually proved fatal, did not discourage him. In one of his final poems, "The Pretty Red-Head," he stated that "without worrying about this war," he foresaw a much greater struggle between the traditionalist and the intellectual adventurer; in ardent terms he bids the reader to allow the pioneers of new fires, new colors and new phantasms, to work on the "frontiers of the limitless," and produce a new reality.

It is true that although the dying Apollinaire's last poems were of courage, power, and victory, the initial manifestations of the younger men who formed the first post-war literary movement, *Dada,* consisted of outbursts of nihilism. But it became so quickly evident to the members of the movement that negation was non-creative, that they buried Dada with much pomp and ceremony. And with the birth of surrealism, creativity became indeed the slogan.

The surrealists set out to revitalize matter, to re-situate the object in relation to themselves so that they would no longer be absorbed in their own subjectivity. In fact, instead of abstracting the object, instead of emptying it of its physical attributes, they decided to add to its qualities through their ability to *see*. A strange identification took place between the see-er and the seer. Seeing was no longer considered a receiving process but an interchange between subject and object. With conscious training, the senses were to reach a point of acuity whereby their function would not be limited to accepting and storing sensations. It would be aimed at enriching the objects of their perception. The essential modernism of the surrealists is their concept of art as a building process, not as an expression or statement of existence as it is, but as a modification or an addition to it. They caught the tone of victory in the last poems of Apollinaire and tried to perpetuate it. René Crevel in his provocative surrealist essay, *L'Esprit contre la raison* (The Mind against Reason) said: "Is it not for the mind a truly magnificent and almost unhoped for victory, to possess this new liberty, this leaping of imagination, triumphant over reality, over relative values, smashing the bars of Reason's cage, and bird that it is, obedient to the voice of the wind, detach itself from earth to soar higher, farther . . . O, wonderful responsibility of poets. In the canvas wall they have pierced the window of Mallarmé's dream. With one thrust of the fist they pushed back the horizon and there in the midst of space have just discovered an Island. We touch this Island with our finger." Their tone of determined optimism is not duplicated by any other contemporary philosophy or art. In this guise, the force and vitality inherent in surrealism make of it the art-concept most in keeping with the productivity of the scientific age in which it has flourished.

The surrealists refused the lonely world of the agnostic, as well as the religious comfort of earlier ages. They also rejected the lulling of the senses produced in the self-imposed vacuum of the latter-day symbolists with their dead mountains, dry sterile thunder, decays and arid plains. René Crevel rejoiced that "Poetry which delivers us of the symbol sows liberty itself." [7]

In one of his most brilliant articles, called "The Marvelous against the Mysterious," André Breton attributes symbolism's weakness to its confusion of the mysterious with the marvelous. For him, it was a sign of default to create through verbal ambiguities an ersatz air of mystery. For him this is a pseudo-mysticism which lacks the power of survival, whereas communion with the marvelous opens to the writer the source of eternal communication with men. As time passes, this gap between symbolist and surrealist inspiration appears to become more and more evident. In one of his more recent articles, "The Ascending Sign," (1947) appearing in the collection of essays, *La Clé du Champ,* André Breton separated the new poet in no uncertain terms from his nineteenth-century counterpart. He vigorously rejected "the end of the world" attitude of his elders. "I do not feel in the least embarrassed to say that today we want no more of this end of the world. We have seen along what lines it has taken shape, and unexpected as it may be, we are struck by its absurdity. We feel only repugnance for this universal swooning." He condemns the artist's adherence to such an attitude as an inexcusable error. In the face of personal as well as national and universal calamities, Breton's unflinching faith in the potential of mankind is the more eloquent and can be explained by his overwhelming belief in the mystery and miracle of art.

True to Mallarmé's premonitions, the surrealists have seen the marvelous in the contradictions of reality. According to Louis Aragon in *Le Paysan de Paris* (1926), the only inconceivable idea is that of absolute limit. The metaphysical point of view should be a daily and essential preoccupation of the artist who must not surrender his conquests to a "supernatural" world. According to him, the true metaphysician does not attempt to hide or transcend the object but seeks to reveal it more fully. The metaphysical preoccupation of the artist must be directed toward knowledge of the concrete entities situated within his sensory orbit. "An object was being transfigured before my eyes, it was not assuming an allegoric shape, nor a symbolic character; it was actually becoming that idea. Thus it infiltrated deep into the earthy mass. I felt the keen hope of touching one of the locks of the universe: suppose the bolt was suddenly to give." He sees a mass of wax in a beauty parlor display and to him it appears to be quivering with all kinds of possibilities, a mannikin with arms crossed on its breast and its dishevelled hair seeking undulations in a crystal cup full of water, a fur store, an electroscope with golden leaves, opera hats, sometimes nothing more than a speck of dust strategically placed; each such object bewitched his imagination and persuaded him that he must shape the infinite from among these finite manifestations of the *universe*. In so doing he would be attuned to the modern spirit. But to do this he had to rise above logic and conscious reasoning, and in the intuitive search for the infinite he would approximate the mystical state of mind of the creators of myths. He came to the conclusion that "man is full of gods, like a sponge immersed in deep heaven."

In the surrealist concept of art, the human condition demands this high dose of mysticism. As one looks back upon the past fifty years of philosophical and literary expression the mystical potential inherent in the writings of the surrealists and their spiritual kin appears to be their most striking distinction. It is indeed their basic motivation. They demonstrate by the miracle of their visions to what degree of intensity modern man can be imbued with mysticism even when in apparent combat against "ancient myths." It is a mysticism which not only accepts the concept of infinity, but has enriched it with the full exercise of the imagination which the surrealists have spent their entire lifetime cultivating and expanding. If their mystique of the image and the object remains elusive as yet to the English speaking world it is because unfortunately English poetic language is still clotted with symbolist verbalisms. Except for a number of translations successfully handled by a few poets,[8] surrealist poems, transfigured into symbolist poems in their English versions, will have to wait for the English language to undergo that same revolution which under the surrealist influence transformed French as a poetic language.

But the surrealists, rising as they do above artistic considerations, transcend in a sense the language barrier. Surrealism is more than art, it is a way of life. It has, as André Breton reaffirmed in his latest writings, a "triple objective" far surpassing literary aspirations: "to transform the world, change life, remake from scratch human understanding." It becomes more and more evident to him that "it is high time man be given a greater awareness of his destiny." So he concludes in an article, written in the Antibes in February 1948,[9] in which he reasserts the surrealist faith in man and in life despite the world disasters of the recent past and the precariousness of the future. As science opens the gates to outer space, the effort of the surrealists to push back the frontiers of creative thinking becomes more meaningful to the modern mind. The scientists' thrust outward toward new physical combinations is in the same spirit as the endeavors of the group of surrealist poets and artists and their forerunners who probed the depths of the human spirit seeking to create a more dynamic and dazzling concreteness.

N O T E S

1. In André Breton's famous article, "Le Merveilleux contre le mystère," which can be found in his collection of essays called, *La Clé des champs,* Les Editions du Sagittaire, Paris, 1953.

2. See for a development of the subject of the relationship of Blake to modern French poetry in my article, "The Literary Fortune of William Blake in France," *Modern Language Quarterly,* September, 1956, pp. 261-272.

3. Charles Baudelaire, *Les Paradis artificiels,* Poulet-Mallasis, Paris, 1860, p. 54.

4. In this study Symbolism with the capital S will refer to the French literary school of the period 1885-1895, while it will be written with the small "s" when designating the general characteristics of the form found in works which lie chronologically and geographically outside of the specific literary school.

5. An astounding work by Charles Chassé, *Les Clefs de Mallarmé*, Aubier, Paris, 1954, would also remove Mallarmé in matters of language from the strictly Symbolist fold. The author claims that Mallarmé wrote with the Littré dictionary as his constant guide in his search for unusual connotations for the simplest words. Mr. Chassé suggests that herein lies a basic difference in style between Mallarmé and the Symbolists for unlike the Symbolists who in general are enticed by rare vocabulary, it is through the plainer words of the language that with the aid of Littré, so says M. Chassé, Mallarmé was able to create his extraordinary effects.

6. A fuller analysis of *Igitur* can be found in my earlier book, *Literary Origins of Surrealism*, Columbia University Press, New York, 1947.

7. René Crevel, *L'Esprit contre la raison*, Cahiers du Sud, Marseille, 1927.

8. As examples of translations which have achieved successful language parallels see Karl Shapiro's rendition of Baudelaire's "La Géante," or Allen Tate's "La Charogne" in Jackson Mathews' collection of Baudelaire translations in his American edition of *The Flowers of Evil*. (New Directions, New York, 1955.)

9. André Breton, "La Lampe dans l'horloge," in *La Clé des champs*, pp. 116-130.

◖

lautréamont's battle with god

When in 1938-9 a poll was taken of contemporary French poets and critics by the periodical *Cahiers G.L.M.* to determine the twenty "indispensable" poems of all time, the name which ranked third among the poets before 1900 and was surpassed only by Rimbaud and Baudelaire, was that of Isidore Ducasse, self-styled Comte de Lautréamont. But what is even more impressive than this is the fact that those who singled him out generally rated him first. Four major surrealists, Eluard, Breton, Soupault, and Péret so designated him, and chose him, not for a single passage or excerpt, but for his whole work considered as a unit and as a milestone in literary history. The surrealists have not been the only champions of this poetic youth who died at the age of twenty-four; but it was they who first considered him a major French poet, although he was technically neither French nor a "poet." He was born in Montevideo of French parents. Arriving in France to study at the Ecole Polytechnique, he wrote in prose, only to prove more convincingly than ever before that the essence of poetry resides not in rhyme but in rhythm, whereby the word pattern expresses a pace of thinking different from that of other forms of writing.

In his preface to Lautréamont's works, Philippe Soupault, one of the original and most faithful members of the surrealist coterie, wrote in overwhelming adoration: "One does not judge M. de Lautréamont. One recognizes him, and in saluting him one bows to the ground." [1] For a time second to Rimbaud as a motivating force for modern poetry and art, Lautréamont has gradually moved up to the first rank, if one is to judge by the sustained and uninterrupted allusions to him since 1920 in the critical comments of modernists in both poetry and art. [2] Editions of his works have multiplied, one of the most recent illustrated by the surrealist artist, René Magritte. In his recent critical works André Breton has Lautréamont's name constantly on his lips as a major influence, and in his *Entretiens* (1952) he interestingly raises the importance of both Rimbaud and Lautréamont above literary classifications. It is, he says, their primary concern for the human condition, their spiritual torment, that lifts them above the literary scene of their time and produces their affinity with later writers. In his preface to the excerpt from Lautréamont's writings which he has included in his *Anthologie de l'humour noir,* Breton signals Lautréamont as a torch blazer: "The most audacious things that for centuries will be thought and undertaken have been formulated here in advance in his magic law."

Lautréamont's imagery, its hallucinatory force, the subconscious train of thought which it reveals, its occasional basis in the absurd create a point of contact with the surrealists. But it is his moral and spiritual perspective more than these literary manifestations of change that indicated a major departure from his contemporaries and brought him closer in line with twentieth-century aesthetic and philosophic thought.

Lautréamont's work is closely involved with the spiritual upheaval caused by the theory of evolution in the second half of the nineteenth century. This scientific event proved as disturbing to that epoch as non-euclidian geometry has been to our own era.

The theory of evolution was welcomed in France by biologists; the philosophers saw in it a dislocation in moral values. The notion of the soul seemed to be put in jeopardy. This moral shock and its inevitable effect upon religious orientation supplied the major impetus for Lautréamont's writings, for his venom, his rejections, his diffidence, and eventually served as a provocation for his wry, dark humor in facing up to the universe and its Creator.

Ducasse was fourteen years old when *The Origin of Species* was published and was still living in Uruguay with his French parents. (His father, a subscriber to various periodicals including *La Revue des Deux Mondes,* kept himself informed of the intellectual news of Europe and particularly of France.) We know very little about the life and intellectual development of this mystifying stranger, the outsider of nineteenth-century French literature; unfortunately he kept no adolescent's diary and died before the age an author takes to his journal. He left no bibliography of his readings, and he disdained memoirs as a literary genre. But judging from the abundant literary allusions of his final fragments called *Poésies,* he was extremely well read for his years and as familiar with English literature as with French. We also know that he showed definite scientific aptitude as a youngster, and after five years of preparatory work in French lycées, went to Paris in 1865 to register in the Ecole Polytechnique. Many a scientific allusion in *Les Chants de Maldoror* points to an interest in technical instruments, in advances in physiology. Moreover he reveals an amazing knowledge of zoology and its terminology, which for the first time becomes a predominant part of the poetic vocabulary.

Since 1845, when Auguste Comte had disturbed men's minds by placing humanity within the order of physiochemical phenomena, France had been in the throes of a philosophical crisis. The publication of *The*

Origin of Species in 1859 intensified the dispute over the biological as opposed to the metaphysical concept of human existence. The French periodicals of the time are filled with polemics on the subject. Langel, a well-known writer of scientific articles for *La Revue des Deux Mondes* wrote in the April 1, 1860 number about the curiosity, criticism, and admiration which Darwin's book had aroused in France.[3] He realized the bitter reaction the book would create. Those who saw in it primarily an attempt to prove man's relation to the ape would reject it with anger without examining it any further. Another writer for the same periodical, A. de Quatrefoges, referred to Darwin in a series of articles entitled "Histoire naturelle de l'homme" (Dec. 15 '60-Feb. 15 '61) and called *The Origin of Species* a "remarkable book." In his opinion it disclosed the impartiality of nature's check and balance system which allowed no one species to overrun the world.

From the point of view of its influence on literature, the most significant aspect of the French reception to Darwin's work was that there appeared less concern with the scientific accuracy of the theory *ipso facto* than with its philosophical implications. According to Ernest Renan, Darwin had taken the first steps toward unraveling the basic philosophical enigma of creation. Referring to Darwin in his article, "Avenir des sciences naturelles," one of a series he did for *La Revue des Deux Mondes,* entitled "Les Sciences de la nature et les sciences naturelles," he envisaged the changes that would have to occur in the study of zoology and asserted that the nonstatic character of existing forms, which Darwin supposes, places his "hypotheses" "incontestably on the path of the great explanation of the world." [4] Henceforth the only true philosophy would be one which accepts this new zoological reality.

It is in this same philosophical vein that the French translator of the book had interpreted the magnitude of Darwinism. Authorized by Darwin himself in 1861, the translation had been undertaken by Clémence Royer, whom Darwin described in one of his letters as "one of the cleverest and oddest women in Europe; is an ardent Deist and hates Christianity, and declares that natural selection and the struggle for life will explain all morality, nature of man, politics." [5] He also pointed out—and this is the most significant part of his comment—that the translator had added footnotes and "in many places where the author expresses great doubt, she explains the difficulty, or points out that no real difficulty exists." In other words through her translation the French public was presented with *a more absolute doctrine* than those who read the original. Mlle. Royer added not only footnotes but a long and militant introduction which championed Darwinism and advertised the book as "a work which will assume the importance of a revolution," [6] in the history of science. She lent further authority to her statements by asserting that Mr. Darwin had written to her saying that she had "understood the general spirit of his doctrine better than his other critics or translators." In her lengthy introduction she emphasized the Darwinian concept of gradual change from beast to man and in the

expression "slowly and progressively by a long series of
varieties, more and more human," [7] used the word "human" in a manner that rings of a dramatic rather than a
scientific verity. Stressing the indication of the slow progress of human development, she claimed that this theory
encompassed a philosophy of nature and a philosophy
of humanity. She opened for re-examination an ominous
question—the theological and philosophical problem of
sin in the light of Darwin's concept of *ascent* as opposed
to the Christian doctrine of *the fall* of man. Thus, reading
her introduction, her readers would feel themselves confronted not only with what she calls the most far-reaching
thing done in the natural sciences, but with what she
termed a very synthesis of the laws of economics, social
sciences and the fundamental code of ethics of all time
and all places. In the preface to the second edition, which
appeared in France in 1866, she assumed credit for having predicted the success of Darwinian doctrine in the
world of science. She claimed that in France no one dared
any longer to oppose it, that many of its earlier critics had
reversed their stand and that it had received the support
of the younger writers, particularly those who "have deserted the opposition to take up the defense." [8]

There is no direct mention of Darwin or evolution in
Lautréamont's work, but in view of the intense interest
in Darwinism between 1860 and 1869, and considering
the youth's general intellectual awareness, his tremendous capacity for reading, and particularly his scientific
tendencies, it takes no stretch of the imagination to assume that Isidore had learned of Darwinism at least as

much as—if not more than—an alert youth of today knows about nuclear physics. In *Les Chants de Maldoror* the primary concern of the author is the reorganization of the living world, biologically integrated and by the same token bereft of the moral supremacy of man. It is even likely that he was thinking of Darwin when he said: "As I write this, new tremors are traversing the intellectual atmosphere: all we need is the courage to face them." [9] This sentence taken out of context has often been quoted as evidence of Lautréamont's awareness of new literary trends. But it is much more likely that he was thinking of the sciences rather than literature for the sentence comes as a conclusion to a passage in which he makes a purely biological analogy between the graftings done on animals and the physiological possibilities of identification between the reader and the author.

Darwinism and the positivist atmosphere in which it flowered affected the work of Lautréamont in the same way that the theory of the Great Chain of Being influenced the Romanticists. From plant to animal, from animal to man, from man to the angel, from the angel to God had been the graded path to perfection as visualized by pantheist writers such as Victor Hugo. In his metaphysical poem, *Dieu,* Hugo made animal, man and the angel plod on their way toward the discovery of the infinite, each according to his relative spiritual capacity. Although a general relationship was sensed by the Romanticists between the other species and man, the proportion between nothingness and perfection was considered entirely different for the inferior forms of life as compared with that in man, and therefore man's belief in his superiority was not shaken. But with Darwinism the scale of gradual per- fectibility was disturbed, for each species was considered perfect in its own fashion. But if we then move from the biological concept of perfection to its philosophical im- plications, man's aspiration toward the absolute is blocked by the very reshuffle of the biological role which promises him only the dark mystery of disappearing as easily and irrevocably from the face of the earth as a fly or a butterfly. Finding himself a descendant of the ape and a brother to the leech, man can no longer believe himself created in the image of God.

Lautréamont did not come to this notion serenely. En- dowed with a propensity for mysticism, he should have lived in a world which accepted miracles and spiritual revelations equal to the scope of his vast imagination. It was a bitter disappointment for him to discover the ex- tent of man's limitations. Maldoror, the half-man, half- beast hero of his work, wanders day and night without rest or respite, troubled by horrible nightmares and by phantoms that hover about his bed and trouble his sleep. He is tormented by his dual combat with God and with man. Lautréamont and his shadowy protagonist, who serves to exteriorize occasionally his own anguish, are in- dignant at being chained to "the hardened crust of a planet," and of being "imprisoned within the walls of their intelligence." Yet, Lautréamont cannot quench his passion for the infinite. And if it is true that he shares the destiny of the animal, then his own unanswered but un- abated longing for the infinite must exist in the lowliest creatures. Indeed, the dogs that bark must be thirsty for the infinite, "like you, like me, like all the rest of humans. I, even as the dogs, feel the need for the infinite. I cannot, I cannot satisfy this need. I am the son of man and of woman, so I have heard. I am surprised . . . I thought I was more." [10] He is angry with God for not having made him *more*. He chides Him for having committed such a blunder: "The Creator should not have engendered such a vermin." [11] He is equally angry with man for having been fool enough to harbor the illusion of his dignity for so long. When he refers to man as "this sublime ape" there is disdain, sarcasm and regret in the use of the terminology.

A less virile and vigilant young man in the throes of such a spiritual crisis might have sought release from his tension by escape, either in terms of physical or intellectual evasion. The examples of such culminations to revolt are numerous in literature. The originality of Lautréamont and the very thing which endeared him to a future generation of artists, is his refusal to be diverted from his intellectual dilemma. Art did not mean to him a form of consolation or a palliative, but on the contrary a confrontation of the problem, a search, perhaps a revelation however painful it might be.

Les Chants de Maldoror attests to Lautréamont's facing up to the tremendous rearrangement of a world in which man is to be considered a material organism and therefore conditioned by the same non-moral impulses as the beasts. This is not really an attitude of revolt, for revolt implies refusal to accept. Young Isidore accepts a totally earth-

bound condition: "The stone would long to escape from
the laws of gravity. Impossible!" But he accepts it with
repugnance as he sets out to portray man through the
eyes of his disillusionment: "Let my war against man be
eternal since each recognizes in another his own degra-
dation." [12] No longer are vestiges of the sublime qualities
of man to be seen in the animal, as the Romanticists had
believed; but on the contrary the undesirable or ugly aspects of animals are mirrored in human beings. Lautréamont begins with a hideously unflattering picture of the
dear reader, calling him a monster, referring to his mouth
as a snout and comparing his movements to those of a
shark. Human eyes are like a sea-hog's, circular like a
night bird's. When man stretches his neck it looks like
a snail's; his legs remind Lautréamont of a toad's hind
limbs. Man's facial expressions are those of a duck or a
goat, his baldness that of a tortoise shell, his nakedness
that of the worm. The cries of a dog, a child, a cat, a
woman have a definite kinship in his picture of the universe.

The analogies between man and beast form the core
of his imagery in *Les Chants de Maldoror.* The similarity
is by no means limited to physical attributes. Human
movements and attitudes are often drawn into very complicated mental associations with animal behavior: "Just
like the stercoraceous, birds that are restless as if always
famished, enjoy the polar seas, and venture only acciden-
tally into more temperate zones, like them I was uneasy
and dragged my legs forward very slowly." [13] Here is his
concept of a human state of mind: "The mind is dried up

by a condensed and continually strained reflection, it howls like frogs in a swamp, when a band of ravenous flamingos or famished herons fall upon the weeds of its shores." [14] He compares the style of a writer to "an owl serious unto eternity." By accepting a close link between man and other living organisms in his metaphors, he destroys old aesthetic values; beauty becomes for him something entirely unorthodox: "He seemed beautiful like the two long tentacle shaped filaments of an insect," or "The beetle, beautiful as the trembling of the hands of an alcoholic." [15] It is farfetched analogies such as these which André Breton has called the surrealism of Lautréamont. The following image has become famous because of the number of times it has been cited as the perfect surrealist image: "The vulture of the lambs, beautiful as the law of arrestment of the development of the chest in adults whose tendency to growth is not in relation to the quantity of molecules that their organism assimilates, vanished into the high reaches of the atmosphere." [16] Even death has a beauty likened to a characteristic of the animal: "Each one has the common sense to confess without difficulty that he does not perceive at first a relation, no matter how remote, which I point out between the beauty of the flight of a royal kite, and that of the face of a child, rising sweetly above an open casket, like a water-lily piercing the surface of the waters." [17]

If man's physical characteristics are akin to those of the animal, his social behavior can also be seen to derive from that of the lower forms of life. Man's social incompatibility, for instance, becomes as natural a phenomenon as that of various species of fish that practice their own brand of isolationism in ocean habitats: "Aged ocean, the different species of fish that you nourish have not sworn fraternity to each other. Each species lives by itself. The temperaments and conformities which are at variance in each one of them, explain, in a satisfactory manner, what at first appears to be only an anomaly. It is thus with man, who does not have the same excuses. When a piece of land is occupied by thirty million human beings, they think themselves compelled not to bother with the existence of their neighbors, stuck like roots on the adjoining piece of land." [18]

The theory of evolution accorded Lautréamont a means of reexamining moral issues. In Mlle. Royer's translation of Darwin, the universal and inevitable destructiveness in all nature was eloquently brought out: "a law of inevitable destruction decimates, either the young or the old, at each successive generation, or only at periodic intervals." [19] In line with this basic struggle for survival described by Darwin, the translator's introduction pointed out that if destruction is a basic law of nature, then the fundamental rule of morality would be the efforts of each species for self-preservation. The recognition of the brutal origin and the biological universality of evil is a basic theme of Les Chants de Maldoror. Lautréamont accepts man's sinful inclinations as the same type of manifestation as the eagle's instinct to tear up his prey. The judges of man's cruelty to man are no other than the eagle, the crow, the pelican, the wild duck, the toad, the tiger, the whale, the shark, or the seal, for he has surpassed the cruelty of all of these.

If man is physically and spiritually no more than a sublime ape, then the angel cannot be very far from this same stage; he appears to Maldoror in the guise of a crab and laughs like a lamb. As the concept of gradual perfection is minimized, even God is divested of his sublimity.

Once the physical and moral characteristics of human beings have been reduced to the level of those of the animals, there remains only one reason for man's greater unhappiness as compared with the attitude of other living organisms on earth: it is the illusion he has of his superiority. In his own moment of disillusionment, therefore, Lautréamont seeks to reduce human pride and thereby find peace through a fraternization with the animal world and finally through actual metamorphosis. He discourses with the greatest of ease with animals (among whom are some of the principal characters of his work): the snake, the beetle, the toad. He seeks a bond with the most despicable of animals: the vampire is his friend, the scorpions his companions; he makes love to the female shark, is consoled by the serene and majestic toad.

The pantheists had also felt a certain affinity with all created beings, but the bond had been considered hierarchic, and man's love of God's other creatures placed on a somewhat patriarchal plane. In Lautréamont's vision of the universe, however, the fraternization of man with beast, Maldoror's actual intercourse with animals, are based on a sordid form of democracy and a powerful atavism whereby man seeks justification for his instincts and attitudes by putting them on a par with those of the lowest forms of animal life.

Maldoror achieves complete identification with the other species. With joy he lives as a shark, or a hog, or a pretty cricket: "The metamorphosis never appeared to my eyes as anything but the high and magnanimous reverberation of perfect happiness for which I had been waiting a long time." [20] He envisions with equanimity two brothers changed into a single spider. Going one step further, he contemplates the possibility of new species: he sees himself as a hybrid, half-bird, half-man, or he imagines with scientific precision a man with the appendages of a duck in close communion with water life: "I saw swimming in the sea, with large duck's feet in place of the extremities of the legs and arms, bearing a dorsal fin proportionally as fine and as long as a dolphin's, a human being, with vigorous muscles, and which numerous schools of fish (I saw, in this procession, among other inhabitants of the waters, the torpedo, the anarnak of Greenland and the horrible scropene) followed with the very ostensible marks of the greatest admiration . . . The porpoise, who have not, in my opinion, stolen the reputation of good swimmers, could hardly follow from afar this amphibian of a new species." [21] In still another instance, his disgust for mankind makes him assume partially the shape of a swan and live at peace with the fish. "Providence, as you can see, has given me in part the organism of a swan. I live in peace with the fish, and they procure the food which I need." [22]

It is significant to note the difference between these metamorphoses and the *Metamorphosis* of Kafka. Gregor Samsa, transformed into a tremendous insect feels nothing but contempt and fear in his new condition. He senses an eternal barrier between himself and humanity. His metamorphosis symbolizes his exclusion from the rest of society, his tremendous loneliness that nothing can cure. On the contrary, Lautréamont feels no disgust; to him the tentacles of an insect are beautiful. It is, rather, the return to his former shape that he considers a misfortune. His metamorphosis is not the terrible thing it is in Kafka's story, but an affront to that human hypocrisy he cannot tolerate. Basically, then, he is not such a pessimist as Kafka for he finds relief from his dissatisfaction with humanity —unwholesome though the manner may be—through his identification with other forms of life.

Nonetheless Lautréamont's attempts to take man down from his self-appointed pedestal and to integrate him with a more closely knit animal kingdom produce a tragic note throughout his writings. Although on the one hand he concedes a dreary sort of materialism that endows man with as little immortality as a butterfly, his innate spirituality produces undertones of a protest against a totally materialistic concept of life as pungent as his determined intent to undermine the traditional faith in human superiority.

The mood fluctuates between insolence and derision on

the one hand, and on the other, the despair of Adam chased from paradise. Although he was obsessed by the seeing of the animal in man, he did not achieve a total portrayal of man as a beast. Even in comparing Maldoror's crime to that of the eagle he unconsciously pointed to the great difference by adding: "yet as much as my victim, I suffered." For all his self-imposed materialism he could not rid himself of the notion of immortality. The very evil he saw in man and in beast he explained by their common rage against the inability to fathom the absolute. Although he humiliated God before his creatures he could not deny His omnipresence. And although man and beast are pictured as being equally ephemeral yet there exists for all a paradise, described in eloquent terms by brother toad who will share it with Maldoror.

Lautréamont died too young to have reached any philosophical conclusions. The ultimate picture which *Les Chants de Maldoror* leaves is twofold. True, on the one hand there is the image of man on a plane little (if at all) above that of the beast. But at the same time Lautréamont's tableau of the animal world is endowed, through his longing for fraternity, with the human qualities he would deny: wisdom, kindness, sympathy, at times even a certain "douceur." As a result his apostrophes to the lowliest creatures, touched as they are with an undercurrent of pathos and compassion, transform many a passage of the work from a derision of mankind to a mockery of those who would deny man any powers beyond those of animals. "I thought I was more than that!" is the chant that soars above the absurd fraternizations. The bold manner in which Isidore Ducasse came to grips with "the great problem of life," whether he lent the prodding to his alter ego, the brother of the leech, or took it upon himself directly, gave his work a universal and timeless character, and set the tragic but unresigned tone, characteristic not of his age but of a future one.

N O T E S

1. See for centemporary judgments in detail on Lautréamont in *Oeuvres complètes,* José Corti, 1953 edition. It includes the successive prefaces by Breton, Soupault, J. Gracq, R. Caillois, and M. Blanchot, which appeared in earlier editions of the work. See also Aragon, "Contribution à l'avortement des études maldororiennes," *Le Surréalisme au Service de la Révolution,* Vol. II, p. 22.

2. The only significant antagonism to Lautréamont in the twentieth century has been Camus' critical article, "Lautréamont et la banalité," which appeared in 1951 in *Cahiers du Sud.* An indignant Breton takes offense at the article and chides Camus for considering Lautréamont "a guilty adolescent." See "Sucre Jaune," pp. 250-53 of *La Clé des Champs.*

3. "Nouvelle Théorie d'histoire naturelle": *L'Origine des espèces, Revue des Deux Mondes,* XXVI, p. 647.

4. E. Renan, *Revue des Deux Mondes,* October 15, 1863, XLVII, p. 765.

5. Charles Darwin, *Letters,* p. 179.

6. Clémense Royer, *De l'Origine des espèces, traduit en français avec l'autorisation de l'auteur.* (2e edition 1866) Guillaumin et Cie, Victor Masson et fils, Paris, p. vi.

7. *Ibid.*

8. *Ibid.,* p. iv-v.

9. Ducasse (Lautréamont) *Les Chants de Maldoror* (Viau) p. 173, the translations from the French here as elsewhere are mine.

10. *Ibid.*, p. 18.

11. *Ibid.*

12. *Ibid.*, p. 139.

13. *Ibid.*, p. 175.

14. *Ibid.*, p. 182.

15. *Ibid.*, p. 180.

16. *Ibid.*, p. 195.

17. *Ibid.*

18. *Ibid.*, p. 21-22.

19. Royer, *op. cit.*, p. 80.

20. Lautréamont, *op. cit.*, p. 159.

21. *Ibid.*, p. 162.

22. *Ibid.*, p. 167.

◐

saint-pol-roux and the

apocalypse

Among the living he is the only authentic precursor of
the modern movement.—*André Breton, 1925.*

There is no more fantastic figure in all French literature
than Paul Roux, the native of Marseille, who settled on
the shores of Brittany, in the fairytale chateau of Cama-
ret, and there lived out his long, Druid-like life with the
legends and the children he created. There also he died
in highly tragic fashion in 1940 as a consequence of an
aimless, absurd Nazi pillage of his home after he had
fought off the murderers of his servant and the attackers

of his only daughter, whom he worshipped as a goddess.

When Paul Roux arrived in Paris at the end of the nineteenth century he quickly fell into the ecstatic atmosphere of the Symbolist *cénacles* and decided to sublimate himself and his mission on earth by transforming his name into Saint-Pol-Roux. However, as he did not manage to fit into any category or genealogy of the Symbolists amidst whom he developed his own quality of talents, he was left out of its annals and completely overlooked by literary critics and historians until the surrealists claimed him as one of their masters. To this day he holds the distinction of being less known abroad than any other French poet, while the writers of literary manuals are still inclined to relegate his merits to a footnote.

The main reason for this oblivion may be the fact that he eludes academic classification. In the end-of-century pseudo-antithesis between symbolism and naturalism, accompanied by left-over "art for art's sake" aestheticism, Saint-Pol-Roux was the only Frenchman who showed himself able to conciliate realism with the symbolic interpretation of art and to succeed in producing a fusion which he called "ideorealism" or "supernaturalism" which is in fact the nucleus of what was later termed "surrealism." If symbolism was the transfiguration of nature, then Saint-Pol-Roux foresaw a more evolved process, which might be called *metafiguration:* not beyond the figure but a virtual change of it within its own entity. This was in fact the simultaneous acceptance and refusal of reality.

At a time when the "pure" word and the rarefied vistas, and vagueness of vision were the fashion, he reestablished contact with the world, a world not age-weary as seen through the eyes of latter-day romanticists, but one which he imagined to be constantly on the verge of the apocalypse, possessed of multitudinous objects which the poet in the fashion of a Merlin can change into wonders through the enlargement of the range of his vision, through a hallucination of his eardrum, and the use of an inner mirror: "I acquired, then, a fabulous mirror that makes you see within." Thus equipped, he reaches what before the advent of Freudian terminology he called "the isle of the inside of my being" (*L'Enfer familial*).[1]

To explore the relationship between this inner self and the outside world became the substance of his poetic work, much of which appeared in the periodicals of the time, such as the symbolist *Vers et Prose,* and in the *Mercure de France.* These writings, mostly poems in prose, were collected in three volumes between 1885-1900, called *Les Reposoirs de la procession* and subdivided into the beguiling titles: "La Rose et les épines du chemin" ("The Rose and the Thorns of the Road"), "De la Colombe au corbeau par le paon" ("From the Dove to the Crow by way of the Peacock"), and "Les Féeries intérieures" ("The Inner Fairyland"). Although a new edition of them appeared in 1946, they are among the collected works that are hardest to find today even in Paris and practically nonexistent in the bookstores or major libraries of the U.S.[2]

Yet despite the inaccessibility of his works, Saint-Pol-Roux, as a poet's poet, has received the highest tributes from poets such as André Breton and Paul Eluard, and

from critics such as Rolland de Renéville. A selection
of his writings, together with biographical and critical essays have appeared in the collection of *Poètes d'aujourd'hui*
and he is also included in a touching volume by Robert Ganzo called *Cinq Poètes assassinés*.[3]

In work inevitably marked by the imprint of symbolism, what is there that constitutes his modernism? Among
the several descriptions he gave of his heterogeneous collection of pieces, one phrase stands out in particular:
"magics of phenomena." It is the notion already high-
lighted by Rimbaud that the poet is a kind of magician
who, not with the wand but with the word transforms
the monotony of existing reality. Saint-Pol-Roux goes a
step further. For him the only way to compensate for the
loss of faith in the supernatural is to create a new type
of miracle, and to replace the God without by a God
within. The poet is regarded as best able to preserve the
mystic essence and to give it its new direction. At a time
when the poet and his outmoded sense of beauty was
threatened with complete extinction, Saint-Pol-Roux proclaimed, as a self-appointed prophet, the transformation
of the twilight of the poet into a new dawn, in which the
poet possessing his own dose of divinity can shape his
own universe.

"Ended is the time of useless dreams, oh my friend,
all the lies have been lived. No, poet, there is no more
room for the wandering heiress of abolished gods, except
to seek her refuge prudently, in the soul of poets where
alone there is possibility of survival. Desist, then, from

searching anywhere but within yourself, Beauty, exiled from her antiquated heavens." [4]

In a piece called "La Joie," appearing in the part entitled "The Inner Fairyland," Saint-Pol-Roux accused of ignorance those who have not yet realized that "it behooves humanity to be the architect of its own paradise and that to become a happy man is equivalent to being metamorphosed into a god." The supreme duty of man is "to claim for one's own time the distant promises of religions and to make of the future chimera a present reality. Joy means force and health, that is to say, Divinity." [5]

His new spectrum, with one end dipped into the inner self, the other extremity stretching to the farthest reaches of imagined physical frontiers, contains a palette not for an imitative art but for pure creation: "Why say again, not say? why do again, not do? why copy, not create?" he asks in his famous *Poesia*.[6] As he reiterated in terms of an "ars poetica" in the *Mercure de France* of 1913: "the art-formula asserts itself as sur-naturalist—the total work can only be sur-creation or supercreation. The whole future of art seems to be there. It is no longer a matter of evolution, what matters is to convert the known substance into an unforeseen substance, an extraordinary one, and, consequently, to transport tradition out of its centuries of lazy habit, into the arduous path of the infinite." [7]

The rise out of the cloistered circuit of his known world is described in impassioned terms. His release is brought about by the image which serves as a sieve; through its transparency, its open hands, the poet envisages a new elasticity of time, and though motionless, he makes voyages into realms which were yesterday only promises.

This attitude of hope, of strength, and optimism was a far-cry from the tenor of his time, with its brooding unconcern with the outer world, incompatible with nihilism and its egocentric vision. Although there is here an aspiration toward the divine as in Rimbaud, it does not echo his revolt, his spurning of world and of society. Saint-Pol-Roux expounded tremendous faith in the powers of man, and if he asked that man mobilize his imagination it was not for personal apotheosis and for satisfaction of a sterile narcissism. On the contrary, he assumed the guise of a pioneer and in colonizing the absolute he had the concern of all humanity at heart. The dreams of the past seemed vain to him. The poet's main care should be for the future. "Believe me, humanity, which must be your only interest, will find its delights in the exteriorization of your love, and so it is that the death of the chimera will serve as a preamble to the pure truth. Write without fear and proudly for the future." [8] Such was his message as he strained to see over the crest of the turning century and set the tone of expectancy and hope that was to be taken up a few years later by Apollinaire, and passed on to the surrealists: a thin, but unbroken line of faith in the capacities of man's mind, that will some day perhaps be noted as an unusual affirmation of man's distinction in a century widely marked with literary pessimism.

As a "geometrician of the absolute" he invades eternity and entrenches himself like an oasis contrived with

Beauty. He is to fashion countries which he signs into existence, imbues them with his own body fluids and muscle strength. Is this transcendentalism? No, says Saint-Pol-Roux. Transcendentalism means changing the existing substance into something ethereal, whereas what he is striving for is quite the contrary: it is the crystallization of essence, the shaping of the ideal into seizable, concrete values, the miracle turned into reality.

How did he propose to bring this about? Not through mathematics, which today has in this sense produced the poetry of technology. Saint-Pol-Roux, the artist, put his faith in the word, in its liberation from the captivity in which it was held for centuries, in its potential uses, in its multiplications of meaning, in what a few decades later, André Breton was to call "the power of earthquakes." In a pertinent article called "Idéoplastie," dedicated to André Gide, Saint-Pol-Roux pondered on the destiny of words: "The words expressed since the origin of the races become eventually a single, continued evocation which in the course of the ages, gathers virtual forces until the magic power has at last its paroxysm, beings and things which were evoked, cohering, germinate, assume textures, reveal themselves little or much, to populate definitely the solid empire of the senses." [9]

Describing the emancipation of the word in "Le Style c'est la vie," he speculates on the marvels of unexpected word encounters: "The reconciliation of a negative word and an affirmative word would soon engender the miraculous sparkle." [10]

Basing his "ideorealism" on Hegel's admonition that

art must no longer imitate nature, Saint-Pol-Roux went
with his scepter of words on his fervent quest for images
through which he would filter the evidences of his senses.

It must be here admitted that the "master of the image,"
as he has been called by his disciples, did not always fulfill the promises which he made in his aesthetic theories.
Much of the imagery which fills the three volumes of his
Reposoirs, as well as the substantial part of his single,
unperformable, poetic play, *La Dame à la faulx* are in
the symbolist tradition with the narrow parallelism of abstract and concrete vocabulary.

But proceeding from page to page one discovers some
of these miraculous sparkles which gave the old man
with the flowing beard his warm welcome among the
younger generation and earned him the epithet of "magnificent." Before the popularization of psychology he
sensed the hallucinatory power of the irrational and indicated that it was a source of poetical inventiveness to
be tapped. Prying into the abnormalities of the simple-
minded and the insane, he identifies his sight with their
possible vision. In his projection of such images, it must
be noted that he makes illogical juxtapositions, approximation of disproportionate objects, and often accepts on the
same level of reality abstract and concrete qualities; these
are all characteristics that were to form the basis of the
technique of surrealist painting and poetry.

In the vision of the "Simples" he perceives: "A dwarf
Princess marrying a giant king; an explorer in a blue
cloak and under his arm a yellow umbrella, swallowed
up by a crocodile, color of fresh grass; a red Indian fight-

ing desperately inside of the belly-ache of an abominable reptile with oyster shells; and other fearful parodies. In the forefront of the stage, two insane musicians. One beats with rapid percussion on a donkey metamorphosed into a drum." [11]

These absurdities are the manifestations by which the "simple-minded" translate into concrete form their intuition of the beyond. In like manner Saint-Pol-Roux's contact with "Le Fol" [12] is a voyage into the realm of pure metaphysics. In Saint-Pol-Roux's fascination with the sensory and mystical orientation of "Le Fol" there is a preview of the interest which Breton and his colleagues were to show in the behavior of hysterics and of their simulations of stages of insanity. Saint-Pol-Roux's "Fol" is a man who is not losing touch with reality but on the contrary is endowed with the power to make concrete what others consider nonexistent or abstract. He can touch "little bits of nothingness," caress their absent plasticity. He has created his own environment, peopled it with life in such vivid fashion that the visitor is willingly beguiled by him. Noting the satisfaction of the "Fol" the poet wonders if after all the sense of concrete possession of one's dream is not the supreme fortune to which man can aspire.

Perhaps the most constant sources of wonder for the poet were the objects that surrounded him every day—what some years later Aragon was to call "the daily miracle." Now, the romanticist appropriated to his ego the beauty perceived in the object, or he attributed his own spiritual qualities to the object. The symbolist saw a parallel existence between himself and the symbols in physical nature. Saint-Pol-Roux's approach is neither of these. Man's inanimate and human surroundings are a constant source of enrichment to his creative faculties: "The soul gapes before the symphony of things and the apotheosis of beings," [13] he observes in "Le Poète au vitrail." Calling himself a "physical poet" because the things about him are his chief concern, he does not however encompass them in a confining reality. The object is not a target but a volleying agent. "The spectacle of the meanest flower emancipates my eyes, and the entire world invades me in a gush of breeze, and directly I perceive divine Beauty delivered of her priests and of their lies." [14]

With this fixation on things, he devised, before Apollinaire, the poems of "il y a," wherein the objects shape the ideas in a veritable somersault of the metaphor. Two of his poems, "Choses" and "Ondes" create a kaleidoscope of images about them, illogical associations (which a little later on would be called automatic). These images suggest the furnishings of Saint-Pol-Roux's world, enlarged by the dose of mysticism in the poet and by the power of the "emancipated" words which serve as a bridge for him between reality and metaphysics, the winged words that shuttle "between the fairyland and the domain of things."

To what extent he cherished these "things" can be seen by one of his last poems, "To be recited at the Funeral of Poets," [15] in which he bids the gravediggers to be careful with the casket of the poet for it is filled with an infinite variety of things, including living forms and man-made objects, a smile and a rainbow, a laurel and a kiss, a nest and a diadem, trophies and an urn—nondescriptive enumerations, but in their nakedness the words sum up the poet's earthly existence, its richness and its scope.

N   O   T   E   S

1. "L'Enfer familial," *Mercure de France,* May 1892, p. 57.

2. *Les Reposoirs de la procession,* Mercure de France, Paris, 1893. The only place where I have been able to find a copy of this work is at the Maison Française of Columbia University. I was unable to purchase it in Paris.

3. Robert Ganzo, *Cinq Poètes assassinés,* Editions de Minuit, Paris, 1947.

4. "La Suprême Hôtesse," *Vers et Prose,* II, 1905, p. 89.

5. *Les Féeries intérieures, Les Reposoirs,* Vol. III, *Mercure de France,* Paris, 1907, p. 49.

6. *Ibid.,* p. 262.

7. "Réponse périe en mer," *Mercure de France,* 103, p. 656.

8. "La Suprême Hôtesse," *op. cit.,* p. 90.

9. *La Rose et les épines du chemin, Les Reposoirs,* Vol. I, pp. 51-2.

10. *De La Colombe au corbeau par le paon, Ibid.,* Vol. II, p. 175.

11. "L'Ame saisissable," *Mercure de France,* 34, 1900, pp. 392-5.

12. *Les Reposoirs,* Vol. I, pp. 240-3; more accessible in *Mercure de France,* 34, 1900, pp. 392-5.

13. *Les Féeries intérieures,* p. 16; more accessible in *Saint-Pol-Roux,* Pierre Seghers, *Poètes d'aujourd'hui,* p. 179.

14. *Ibid.*

15. See *Ibid.,* pp. 208-10.

◐

apollinaire and the

modern mind

An unusual experience in historical self-consciousness must have belonged to those who attained the age of reason with the turn of the century and felt compelled to express awareness of a new era. Dates are arbitrary landmarks, and the world does not alter suddenly because a new figure appears on the calendar. Yet, a reading of the more personal writings of those who experienced the change from the eighteen hundreds to 1900 gives indications of a psychological upheaval and of a conviction on the part of these writers that if things had not changed they should—an attitude not as readily associated with the mid-century adult. The writings of Guillaume Apollinaire, born in 1880, show that he was not only conscious of a transition but felt that he must have a hand in the heralding and shaping of a new world.

Nineteen-hundred brought to France an international exposition. One of the most important gadgets peddled there was the magical electric bulb; it was also the year of the cinema, the Paris subway, and liquid oxygen. It marked the advent of the supremacy of the scientist in the history of human progress, not the *pure scientist* who dealt with the abstract, but the man who applied the principles of science and *produced*. Whatever else twentieth-century man was going to possess in the way of distinguishing traits, he seemed assured of a generous share of concrete intelligence, an inventive spirit, which would provide unfathomable resources to the activity of his imagination.

This development of technical imagination seemed, however, to have no immediate parallel in artistic activities. Art suddenly appeared a weak sister. Since the end of the nineteenth century a rift had taken place between science and art which was growing wider and wider. Art, after a shortlived alliance with positivism, had soon protested, revolted, taken refuge in the dream, unsuspecting that soon science was to claim the dream itself as one of its legitimate domains of investigation. Science seemed to be the destroyer of the marvelous and the mysterious.

The resentment was not untouched by a certain amount of jealousy on the part of the artist in regard to the strides made by the scientific inventor.

This conflict is vividly demonstrated by Apollinaire in his *Le Poète assassiné* (1916). Much of this Rabelaisian novelette is autobiographical. We trace the fantastically confused origin and international upbringing of the poet-hero, Croniamental, which parallels closely the apocryphal data about Apollinaire's own early years. We see the poet making ties with the vanguard painters of his time, like Apollinaire's own relations with the cubists. We are exposed to Croniamental's conception of an extraordinary play containing in a one-paragraph description the seeds of playful irrationality (which was to be more notoriously demonstrated the following year in the staging of Apollinaire's play, *Les Mamelles de Tirésias*):

"Close to the sea, a man buys a newspaper. From a house on the prompt side emerges a soldier whose hands are electric bulbs. A giant three meters high comes down from a tree. He shakes the newspaper vendor, who is of plaster. She falls and breaks. At this moment a judge arrives on the scene. He kills everyone with slashes from a razor, while a leg which comes hopping by fells the judge with a kick under the nose, and sings a pretty, popular song."

Finally Croniamental comes face to face with the arch-enemy of poets, not the smug unimaginative bourgeois, but the champion of the scientists, Horace Tograth, who demands the killing of all poets because they have been overrated and are contributing nothing valuable to present civilization.

"True glory has forsaken poetry for science, philosophy, acrobatics, philanthropy, sociology, etc. Today all that poets are good for is to take money that they have not earned since they seldom work and since most of them (except for cabaret singers and a few others) have no talent and consequently no excuse. . . . The prizes that are awarded to them rightfully belong to workers, inventors, research men. . . ."

Croniamental protests furiously against this persecution of the artists, and pays with his life. Yet Apollinaire leaves an undertone of criticism directed not exclusively against the philistine debaser of the poet, but also against the artist in general who has partially merited the attack. He indicates that the fault for this apparent impotence of poets is partly the public's, that public which demands boredom and unhappiness as the subject matter of literature instead of magic such as is expected of the modern scientist and even of the simple acrobat. As for Cromiamental, he is Apollinaire's concept of the authentic twentieth-century artist, one who has looked God in the face: "I am Croniamental, the greatest of living poets. I have often seen God face to face. I have borne the divine refulgence which my human eyes made softer. I have lived eternity."

He is killed by the science worshipper, who does not realize that Croniamental is not a stereotype poet. His sculptor friend, cognizant of the hard times through which poets are passing, manages to build him a statue,

an extraordinary one, "a profound statue made of nothing," ironically symbolic of the emptiness of art and glory,
also indicating that the true quality of the poet is indis-
tinguishable to ordinary eyes.

Although in *Le Poète assassiné* the conflict between
science and art ends in tragedy and defeat for the artist,
Apollinaire defied in his own life and writings the secondary role attributed to the artist in the world of new
values. He sought a conciliation between the work of the
scientist and of the modern artist. He called himself and
those like him "pilgrims of perdition" because they were
risking what intellectual security they had as artists to explore the uncertain and the unproven. Although his conjectures about the potentialities of the modern mind were
most precisely stated in an article, "L'Esprit moderne,"
which appeared in the *Mercure de France* in 1918 shortly
after his death,[1] he had been crystallizing these views
since his earliest associations with the artistic and literary
coteries of Paris.

The need for inventiveness to preserve the prestige of
the twentieth-century artist in competition with the twentieth-century technologist was first illustrated through
Apollinaire's negative reaction to the existing imitative
and autobiographical novel much in vogue then in France.
As principal reviewer on the staff of *La Phalange* for a
number of years early in his career, he found ample opportunity to criticize the unoriginality of the novel form.
Even when commending what he considered an ex-
ceptional one such as *Tzimin-Choc* by Louis-Bréon he

makes of it an opportunity to chide the average contemporary novelist for his superficial realism, for his recourse to the easy autobiographical material. And yet he somehow hopes that a change of direction is at hand:

"Wonder should be the primary concern of the novelist, we should abandon for a while—long enough to realize what reality is—all this false realism which overwhelms us in most novels of today, and which is only platitude. Under the pretext of following the trend for psychological and sentimental naturalism, most authors do not even need to have recourse to their imagination any longer. Autobiography is all that is needed, and those who take the trouble to invent the most insignificant little story become famous. They have almost no competition to fear. But things appear to be changing. Imagination seems to be reclaiming its rightful place in literature." [2]

While literature had been neglecting imagination, science had learned to make maximum use of it. It had cast aside the known patterns of matter and through ingenuity had created new ones. Science's contribution, in Apollinaire's opinion, was *its ability to give reality a relative meaning* and thus to liberate it from its assumed synonymity with the *natural*. The unnatural could become a reality, as twentieth-century objects, which had no connection with nature, were proving more conclusively every day. The factory worker was all the time creating reality. The automobile had a dynamic existence which removed Apollinaire from the old world and its limited scope; candidly he states it in his poem, "La Petite Auto":

We said goodbye to a whole epoch . . .
We understood my friend and I
That the little auto had driven us into a
    brand new time
And though we were grown men
We were really born only yesterday
                                        Calligrammes

Why not a parallel between the creativeness of applied
science and that of the arts? In his preface to *Les Mamelles de Tirésias* he fabricated the word "surreal" to desig-
nate the human ability to create the unnatural, and he
pointed out that man's first surrealistic act was the creation of the wheel, which imitates the physical function
of motion but creates a form entirely independent of forms
known to exist in nature. The wheel becomes for him a
product of purely creative work on the part of man, a
manifestation of unconscious surrealism. Now the magic
of the telephone, the automobile, the electric bulb, the
airplane—creations in the same sense as the wheel—dis-
proved even to a further degree the well accepted adage
that there is nothing new under the sun. The same independence from natural objects, which the technologist
had achieved by his inventions, and through which he
revolutionized the physical appearance of the world,
should be sought by the artist in his own medium. To
Apollinaire the acquisition of that freedom was to be the
fundamental attainment of the modern mind. One could
be a poet in many fields, and the technologist had proved
for the moment to be a "poet" in a truer sense than the
artist, admits Apollinaire in "L'Esprit moderne": "Poetry

and creation are one and the same thing; he alone must be called poet who invents and creates, as much as it is given to man to create . . . One can be a poet in all fields: all that is needed is to be adventurous, to go after discoveries."

In retrospect it occurred to him that the poet had until recently been the precursor of the scientific inventor. Had he not conceived of the airplane centuries before the technologist was able to materialize his legend of Icarus? But Apollinaire had to admit that for once the scientist had stepped ahead of the artist in the realm of magic. Since the scientist had become not a destroyer of fantasy but a producer of marvels, his inventiveness should prove a challenge and an incentive to the artist: "The wonders impose on us the duty of not letting imagination and poetic subtleties lag behind those of the artisans who improve the machine. Already scientific terminology is in deep discord with that of the poets. This is an unbearable state of affairs."

Art's pitfalls in recent times had been its imitative approach to nature. Apollinaire waged war against photography, which to him was in all its technical perfection what smoke is to fire. He made photography the symbol of imitation and the antithesis of art. Some years later Louis Aragon was to repeat Apollinaire's words against photography even more vehemently in defining his concept of the relation between reality and art. Since reality, according to Apollinaire's understanding of it, was dependent not on physical nature but on the mind's creativeness, all the arts were long overdue for the same basic revolution: that of creating rather than representing the object.

The symbolists had had a similar notion about the "interiority" of art but they had feared the object, feared the *concrete,* which they had mistaken for the *natural.* To point out the difference Apollinaire made up the word "surreal" as opposed to "symbolist." True to this distinction the culmination of the symbolist attitude was to be abstract art and not surrealism.

Although Apollinaire showed a certain affinity at first with Marinetti and other futurists, he soon noticed something superficial in the way the futurists extolled science. It was the object of scientific creation which interested them rather than the process of creation. Marinetti's attitude toward science is a far cry from Apollinaire's. When in an unfriendly apostrophe to the moon the futurist praises the electric bulb and belittles the light of the moon, he is led to no adventures of the imagination by the stimulus of the newly created object of science but merely expresses a journalistic appreciation of technological progress. In much the same manner, in his *The Pope's Monoplane* the airplane is admired as a means of escape and not as an impetus to broader artistic visions.

Apollinaire's relations with the cubist painters were of a much more fundamental nature. He found in the cubists the truest competitors of the imaginative technologists. As the perfect illustration of his own theories he defined cubism in *Les Peintres cubistes* (1913) as "an art of conception which tends to rise to the level of creation." In looking back on traditional painting he found too many painters who worshipped plants, stones, water and men. Without being iconoclastic—as some of his followers were to become—he warned the artist not to be too much attached to the dead. He foretold before José Ortega y Gasset a dehumanization in art, contended that the true artist tends to be inhuman: "They painstakingly search for the traces of inhumanity, traces which are to be found nowhere in nature."

He discovered in the works of the cubists the fourth dimension of reality, which he deemed not only a proof of creativeness but of divinity. This new dimension was conveyed by simultaneous representations in various perspectives, giving the impression of the immensity of space which overflowed in all directions at the same time and suggested the infinite. The cubists were thereby producing, according to Apollinaire, a fusion of science and metaphysics. Through his observations of the cubists' activities he was able to make a crucial distinction between the new and the old mental formation of the artist: the traditional artist is a sieve of human experiences and, stimulated by the muse, he is a facile interpreter of life; while the new artist, like the scientist, plods from effort to effort in the process of construction, unaided by divine inspiration, but possessing himself the grains of divinity.

Apollinaire's friendship with Picasso, Braque, Picabia and the Douanier Rousseau made him a better apologist for the new art than the painters themselves could have been, thus setting a precedent for closer association between the arts of painting and writing, a relationship which was to prove so significant and influential in the development of dadaism and surrealism.

The influence of ideas is a subtle thing and an elastic one. To what extent an individual is the originator and principal propagator of concepts can be a subjective evaluation. Certainly in the writings of several early twentieth-century thinkers there were to be found parallel definitions of the new objective in the arts. We have noted Saint-Pol-Roux's stress on the creative powers of the poet. Max Jacob, who was Apollinaire's friend and contemporary, gave a similar importance to inventiveness and to the faculty of using concrete imagery in his *Conseils à un jeune poète;* and the gifted young poet, Pierre Reverdy, was seeing in cubism in 1917 much the same thing as Apollinaire and expressing it in almost the same words: "an art of creation and not of reproduction or interpretation." [3] And strangely, in an issue of *La Phalange,* at the time when Apollinaire was its book reviewer, there appeared the translation of an article by the American, Gerald Stanley Lee, explaining the modern writers' fear of the machine and deploring their melancholy attitude toward it. The artist, he said, is afraid of the machine only because he has let himself be dominated by it instead of emulating the attitude of mind which created it. [4] The examples could be multiplied. Apollinaire's importance lies not so much in being the originator of an attitude as in having stated it more provocatively and held to it more persistently than his contemporaries. His ideas on art did not remain in the realm of theories but were illustrated consciously in the major portion of his poetic work.

Apollinaire was not a suggestive artist in the manner of the symbolists. Like the magician that he wished to emulate, the poet tried to infuse his work with unexpected sparks: visions, concretely resplendent and limitless, meant to surprise and mystify the reader in the way that a rabbit is pulled out of a sleeve. The old artistic aim was to arouse the emotions of the reader or spectator; now art was to be a sort of jovial game to create not pity nor empathy, but *wonder*—and sometimes irritation.

His earliest poetical work, *L'Enchanteur pourrissant* (*The Rotting Enchanter*) 1909, in which he depicts the imprisonment of the enchanter by those who exploit his power but also prophesies the magician's eventual resurrection, ends with a piece of writing called "Onirocritique," which is a natural appendix to his work. It represents Apollinaire's earliest example of inventive writing: in an apocalyptic vision of the universe he combines creatures and disintegrates them into a hundred feet, eyes, in an ever-changing panorama; sounds are transformed into beings, silence into movement, trees consume stars; and each reader is left with his own interpretation of the imagery.

In *Alcools* (1913), his first collection of verse, we find instances of the same mixture of perspectives and sensations. Just as the technologist formed a new world of realities with existing matter, Apollinaire believed that words could make and unmake a universe. He attempted to use his "five senses and a few more" to string side by side images often logically disconnected, demanding of the reader leaps and bounds of the imagination to keep pace with his self-characterized "oblong" vision. His dislocations of temporal and spatial perspective defy ordinary reality but are of this earth in their tactility, colors and scents. "Cortège" presents one of the most incoherent yet challenging visions in the theme of the inverted flight of a bird and its effects on the relativity of land, sky and light:

Bird, tranquil in your inverted flight, bird
Who nestles in the air
At the limit of my memory's glare
Shut out with your second lid
Not for the sun nor for the earth
The oblong fire growing in intensity
Until one day all alone it shall prevail

[Oiseau tranquille au vol inverse oiseau
Qui nidifie en l'air
A la limite où brille déjà ma mémoire
Baisse ta deuxième paupière
Ni à cause du soleil ni à cause de la terre
Mais pour ce feu oblong dont l'intensité ira s'augmentant
Au point qu'il deviendra un jour l'unique lumière]

"Le Brasier," "Le Voyageur," "Vendémiaire," could be called experimental poems: attempts to avoid ordinary descriptions of the world and to personalize and thus recreate the realities of fire, sun, sky, sea, heights, depths and the elixirs of human thirst. In "La Maison des morts" (The House of the Dead) he goes as far as to combine the two spheres of life and death, and he allows his living and dead creatures to intermingle and coexperience not abstract but very concrete sensations.

Calligrammes (1918) is a more striking example of his inventive approach to writing. The theme in this collection of poetry is the newness of the world: new fires, new forms, new colors impatient to be given reality. The wand which has brought about the return of the "age of magic" is said to be the war. Despite the tragedy and pathos experienced first hand by Apollinaire, his vigorous imagination accepted in compensation the challenge of new vistas revealed by the inventions pertaining to the war. With prophetic eye he placed the marvels of war above its miseries. Beyond the political conflict he discerned the more fundamental quarrel between tradition and invention. In a poem called "War" he bids his readers not to cry over the horrors of war but instead to realize that, while before we only knew the surface of earth and sea, now we could reach deeper below and higher into space.

He felt the science of war making him at once invisible and ubiquitous. Time had acquired a new flexibility which could make it vanish and be restored. He sensed that man was approaching the exploration of the lower depths not only of the physical world but also of his own consciousness.

In *Calligrammes* Apollinaire used juxtaposition and discarded symmetry and order much more than in his previous works. These poems are circumstantial in the sense that their point of departure is a factual event or concrete detail of the color of the times. But the submarine cables, the planes fighting overhead, the bombs, the flares, the telephone or the phonograph, each serves as an impetus to new imagery surpassing its circumstantial nature and announcing to Apollinaire the need to alert and sharpen the senses.

When Apollinaire was criticized for the obscurity of the symbols in his play, *Les Mamelles de Tirésias,* he defended himself by stating that true symbolism, like the Sibylline Oracles, lends itself to many meanings, "to numerous interpretations that sometimes contradict each other." *Calligrammes* fearlessly illustrates this theory, thereby setting a new relationship between the artist and his audience: if the writer or painter is no longer to be a mere interpreter of life but a creator, then his erstwhile role of interpreter will be transferred to the reader or spectator, who loses his passive task of absorbing and feeling the message of the artist and assumes the more creative role of relating the sensations of the artist to his own experiences and his own faculties of imagination and association. Thus the flexibility of the visions of the artist are set to a perpetual motion of interpretations, which may in themselves be a form of creative activity. This same technique, called by the uninitiated the obscurity of modern art forms, was to become the *sine qua non* of the works of the dadaist and surrealist disciples of Apollinaire.

Perhaps fifty years from now the greatest mark left by Apollinaire on the current of ideas will be the break he dared to make with the *mal du siècle* attitude which had played the poetic strings of melancholy in the nineteenth century, and had then continued uninterrupted through an undetermined state called "inquiétude" or uneasiness over the modern world's ills shared by the leading writers before and after World War I. This attitude which has been deemed by many critics to be synonymous with profundity, had led them, perhaps prematurely, to term the epoch since World War I as the age of anxiety. It may be that when there is the possibility of observing the century with more perspective, the critic will find this noncommittal, indecisive worrymindedness a carry-over from an earlier age, just as the literary forms practiced by many of the highly esteemed writers of the epoch were not a change from those of the nineteenth century but a prolongation of them. Apollinaire is one of the very first to have felt that dejected, introspective brooding could not be a characteristic of the modern mind. "This pessimism more than a century old, ancient enough for such a boring thing," [5] should, he said in *Les Mamelles de Tirésias,* be now replaced. The fat, jovial, buoyant cosmopolite had had his share of disappointments in life, but he always maintained his hope in the future with its challenges and surprises. In the words of his friend Philippe Soupault, who recalled Apollinaire's character after his death, he was "the being most happy to be alive" and although sometimes sad, languorous and melancholy, yet never one who despaired.[6]

Apollinaire believed more fervently perhaps than any writer of his generation in the future of art, and he announced in one of his very last writings, *Couleur du temps,* that the resurrection of the poets was approaching. He wanted to give man confidence in himself, he wanted to counteract the age-old cliché that man has no future, that he is hopelessly ignorant and a born idiot. Having tried to cultivate in himself the power of prophecy he saw beyond the grimness of mechanization, beyond the dumbness of uncontrolled instincts, beyond the gruesomeness of war. He was not afraid to use the word "progress" although he had an inkling that a more appropriate term for what he wanted would be found perhaps in a hundred years. Beyond mechanization was to be the new world of enchanters, beyond uncontrolled instincts would be the discovery of their secret motivations and possibly the eventual improvement of man, beyond the gruesomeness of war would be the letting down of physical barriers, the broadening of the domains of man in all directions—as indeed they have been broadened since World War II. And through all these things, what primarily interested him was the possibility of new subjects for the artists' imagination: thousands of new combinations which spell progress in art, as well as in life. The hymn of the future would be "paradisiac," he said in his poem "La Nuit d'avril 1915," and "victory" had for him a more basic meaning than the cessation of hostilities.

Was Apollinaire's optimism to prove an anachronism in the intellectual history of the twentieth century? Considering the prevailing pessimistic strain in the best known and most acclaimed writers in most countries in the quarter century following Apollinaire's death, and even including some of the post-World War II crop, one is inclined to believe that Apollinaire misjudged the "modern mind." Yet many of his contemporaries and younger *confrères* had the conviction that he would exercise great influence on art and literature. Philippe Soupault called him a "signal flare" on the artistic horizon and pointed out that Apollinaire subjected his contemporaries to a sort of contagion: "It is . . . thanks to him that poetry was revived. . . . All he had to do was to write a poem and immediately many poems would be born, publish a book like *Alcools* and all of the poetry of his time found an orientation." [7] André Breton, who according to Soupault was one of the first to realize what a poet Apollinaire was, grants him the credit of having been the re-inventer of poetry, in his article on Apollinaire in *Les Pas perdus;* and he points to the psychological truth revealed in the apparent disorder of his writings, this disorder which through Breton was to become a major characteristic of modern poetry in France. But awareness of Apollinaire's role as a motivator of ideas went beyond French boundaries. In his preface to Apollinaire's *Il y a,* Ramón Gómez de la Serna states that he was the poet who has suffered the least degree of death in dying.

The group which, despite its initial tone of despair, gradually took up Apollinaire's tone of optimism, was the surrealists themselves. Ironically, in the midst of the tragic social and political chaos of troubled Europe they have increasingly adopted the note of fortified prophecy bequeathed to them by their precursor. The war and postwar poems of Breton, Aragon, Char and Eluard abound in the same type of energetic optimism and hope as in the vigorous poems of Apollinaire written during the previous war.

In the past decade, the dozen or so works that have unraveled Apollinaire's unpublished poems, biographical data and souvenirs of his friends, have been received by the French public as a homage to a national hero. A street has been renamed in Paris to bear his name. The summer of 1952 saw an issue of *La Table Ronde,* dedicated to Apollinaire, sell as popular literature on the kiosks of Paris. In a letter to me shortly after the celebration of the thirtieth anniversary of the poet's death, Madame Apollinaire wrote of "the great enthusiasm and fervent admiration of Apollinaire which animates the youth of today."

For the critic to be prophetic is even more presumptuous than for the creative writer, and yet I venture to ask what can be the utter and outer limits of pessimism in literature? Silence or suicide, both literary dead ends! This brings Apollinaire's prophecy into the category of Pascal's wager. He can be right or wrong. If wrong, no matter, for the line of artists will have extinguished itself. If he is right in believing in the energy of creativeness of the modern mind and in thus establishing a *mystique* of the *here and now,* he is indeed a herald of a new age of enchantment and will loom more and more prodigious in the history of ideas as well as of literature.

Science is never pessimistic about its powers and is never ashamed to foretell beyond its existing limitations its capacity for tomorrow. Perhaps art, following more and more in Apollinaire's footsteps, may rid itself of its apologetic attitude and find, as Apollinaire hoped, that after all the world is just beginning and imagination has yet to come of age.

N O T E S

1. See "L'Esprit moderne," *Mercure de France,* 130 (1er décembre 1918),

2. *La Phalange,* 27 (1908), p. 271.

3. Pierre Reverdy, "Cubisme," *Nord-Sud,* I, p. 6.

4. Gerald Stanley Lee (tr. by Léon Bazalgette), "La Poésie de l'âge des machines," *La Phalange,* 33, p. 789-95.

5. *Les Mamelles de Tirésias,* p. 31.

6. Philippe Soupault, "Guillaume Apollinaire," *La Revue Européenne,* 6 (1er janvier 1926), 3-8.

7. *Ibid.*

F   I   V   E

◐

pierre reverdy

and the materio-mysticism

of our age

Pierre Reverdy has been truly one of the important metaphysical poets of our time. A contemporary of two great
non-realists, Claudel and Valéry, he found spiritual outlet neither in a specific religion nor by reducing life to an
abstract purity. Incapable of public adherences, he has
lived his personal as well as artistic life in the lonely mar-
gins of literary coteries. According to him, life is the same
for everyone, nothing amazing, nothing unpredictable.

His own has been free of personality quirks, of mental or physical aberrations. In fact his art so completely invaded the current of his daily living that biographers would have little to write about him. This is not to say that he has "lived" for his art, but on the contrary his art has been the expression of that life, has comprised its constant pulsation and passage and has been integrated with it. Upon the publication of his first major volume of poetry, *Les Épaves du ciel* (Chips of Heaven), written for the most part between 1915 and 1918, and collected in 1924, this is all the information which he gave about himself: "Pierre Reverdy, born in Narbonne on September 13, 1889. No travel, no adventures, no story, but what stories."

A rapid reading or sampling of his poetry misleads the reader completely: one imagines an ethereal being, Nordic in melancholy, pale with dreaming, misty-eyed with vision, at ease only in the nebulous atmosphere of smoggy cities and cloudy countrysides. The delicacy of certain imagery suggests a frail, almost incorporate being, unsubstantial as some of the mirages inherent in his work.

Yet, this is only the initial step to the understanding of Reverdy and his poetic world; and this is the antithesis of his true self.

In reality, Reverdy is a stocky, robust being, not pale but fiery of look, not delicate of movement but forceful, not fluid of speech or gesture but abruptly energetic, direct of aim, vibrant of purpose, a product not of mist but of the hot sunshine of his Mediterranean birthplace. And a deeper reading of the work reveals a much more concrete world of things and beings, solidity of objects with precise though unaccepted positions, the world in metaphysics, i.e. a mutation of the material world produced by a thirst for mysticism acute and sustained for all his lifespan, his roots in heaven and his hands in clay.

The major biographical and artistic fact in Pierre Reverdy's life was, at the age of twenty, the impact of his father's death; not just the emotional shock of loss of the dearest being in his life, but the horrifying material reality of the metamorphosis between livingness and lifelessness, the abruptness of the change, and the infinite implications it suggested to him in terms of the myths connected with immortality. On that day and forever after he was obsessed by the fixed and morbid idea of nothingness. His spiritual house of cards collapsed, and it is thereafter futile and deceptive to talk of the poet Reverdy in terms of religious mysticism or dogmatic faith. In his prose maxims (1930-36) collected under the title, *Le Livre de mon bord* (1948) he says touchingly and yet bluntly: "One can believe in God without loving him . . . but one can love him without believing in him—with a love, insane, rebellious and strong, loving all that he might have been if he could have been." [1] This is the only love of God that one can honestly refer to in speaking of the mysticism of Reverdy.

Yet, his loss of faith is the beginning of his real spirituality, with which his whole poetic work is inextricably involved. As he abandoned the faith of his childhood he felt that for him faith had been a stopgap in his spiritual development. It seemed to him that belief was the end of a crisis and therefore incompatible with his nature and its need for relentless searching. The loss was really a gain, the beyond had lost its determined target, expanding into something larger, in fact the beyond was henceforth "everything that is outside of the skin that is tightly drawn around our body." He took the "metaphysical distress" that arose out of his personal loss of father and of God not with self-pity but as an impulse towards greatness: "it is not a weakness but on the contrary a symptom of quality and force, for every soul that is besieged by it can henceforth rely only on itself to surmount it." [2]

The loss of faith is the beginning of spiritual fortitude for Reverdy. He accepts the fact that death is the greatest enemy of man and the invincible one. But this fact creates in him neither a sense of defeat nor of cynical disdain. Disdain of death would be accompanied by disdain of life, and although he admits the tragic basis of life he refuses to disdain living. The alternative is to transmute life within our limited number of years. How to transmute it becomes the preoccupation of his life and work.

Reverdy's work is the overflow of this metaphysical quest. If he became a writer it was because that happened to be the only means of expression at his disposal at the moment of spiritual awakening. Had he been trained in art (like his father), or in music, his poetic contacts with the physical world would have been just as readily represented by lines or notes.

From 1915 on, the stratifications of his life,—rather

eventless from the point of view of social involvements or emotional crises,—is the slow unwinding of his work. After his first volume of collected poems, already cited, there was the exposition of his *ars poetica* in *Le Gant de Crin,* and the eventual collection in three volumes of his complete writings, including the previously mentioned *Le Livre de mon bord,* and two volumes that comprise his total poetic writings from 1913 to 1949. Throughout the entire work, whether prose or poetry, the principal theme and thought is the quest for the absolute in the various strata of reality. It is significant to note that although he sidestepped the coterie of the surrealists, he preceded them, then became their contemporary, sharing their metaphysical aspirations; but he evolved his destiny independently and in solitude though remaining on friendly terms with surrealist artists and poets, just as he has been faithful to his earlier affiliation with the cubists without making it a total involvement. Preferring to live in the monastery climate of Solesmes and taking only occasional trips to Paris and its hotbeds of literary theory, he integrated nonetheless within his work the many metaphysical *élans* of concern of the artists of our time.

First of these was the concept of reality. Unlike metaphysical poets of past epochs, Reverdy has always considered reality irrevocably involved with mysticism. His *mystique* does not annihilate reality. Because of this he has often been called a "realist." But we must be careful to understand that what he calls reality is not the accepted concept of the real. For him reality is what lies beyond "the deception of the senses." It is neither on earth nor in heaven, but as he terms it "over the roofs." In his sturdy hands he will take the clay of earthly objects and through language transform them. Were he to abandon the plane of reality, he explains in an essay entitled "Fausses Notes" (False Notes) appearing in the art magazine, *Verve* (1952) he would end up in nothingness. The poet must stay in reality, after having first made a "leap toward the heights, like drops of water, surging out of the river," but only to return, the better "to be absorbed after having thrown off darts of diamonds with which light had adorned them."

According to Reverdy, man's leaps of imagination are valid only when they meet with an equal degree of linguistic power. The literary image, even as the pictorial, has an existence independent of the natural order of things. It is neither a quality of man who created it nor consistent with the objects of this world. It resides outside both the see-er and the objects of his vision, yet has its own inherent reality. "Poetry is neither in life nor in things—it is what you do with them and what you add to them," [3] he reflects in *Le Livre de mon bord*. The only metaphysics possible for him consists in rendering matter dynamic and thereby reaching the absolute through matter.

It can therefore be said that the poet is against reality yet deals constantly with it. When, on the one hand, Reverdy says: "The poet is a furnace in which to burn reality," [4] and in the next breath asserts that "the poet is essentially a man who aspires to the domain of the real," there is not really the contradiction that the words seem to indicate. In a most lively image Reverdy illustrates this apparent contradiction: "The poet is a transformer of current—from the high tension of reality to the incandescent filament which gives light." [5]

In other words, unlike his precursors, the Symbolists, he accepts the exterior world just as he refuses to disdain life, but at the same time he constantly affirms man's insatiable hunger for the marvelous. In this quest, the enemy will not be reality but nature. The distinction which he makes between the two has been accepted as fundamental by the surrealists. Reality is what you make it; physical nature is the inflexible element, and must be surmounted by man's imagination. He says in *Le Livre de mon bord*:

"The innermost quality of man is his inexplicable need for the marvelous. And that is his sharpest point of divorce from nature. We no longer believe in miracles— nothing is more obvious. But the miracles in which we no longer believe are as nothing in comparison with those that each man carries in reserve within his innermost self and which his imagination offers him at all time." [6]

In his acceptance of the exterior world he points up better than any critic of the time the point of default of symbolism. He minimizes the importance of the dream, which had been the crux of the aspirations of both the romanticists and the symbolists. For Reverdy it is only a means to an end: the tunnel that passes under reality, a gutter of reality. The poet dreams, but he dreams of life, of his hypothesis of life, in which he learns to love life better: "One learns to love reality better sometimes after a long detour by way of dreams." [7] His dream then is hard and durable, as the studies in concrete which are the dream realizations of the artist. "It was an unheard of adventure, that of the artists of the concrete, when they extended this domain toward that of poetry, the immense field of the undefinable," he observes in the *Verve* article. It is their example that he chose to follow rather than that of the musician whom the symbolists imitated. In following the techniques of music, poets had met with their most dangerous pitfall,—a danger from which we have not yet (1952) liberated ourselves, deplores Reverdy. For by simulating the only art that does not need to evoke reality, they stumbled into a vagueness not only of expression but of mind: an exit out of life leading not to the infinite but to nothingness.

No, the dream and its imprecisions, may be a temporary opiate to the poet, but he must not become addicted to it, for it will lead to sterile fields. Not the musician but the artist should be the modern poet's counterpart. It is the artist that has succeeded in attaining not an escape but a marvelous kind of new reality through the object.

"If man disappears, the earth remains, the inanimate objects, the stones in the road. If the earth disappears, there remains all that is not the earth. And if all that is not the earth disappears, there remains what cannot disappear—one may wonder why—because one cannot even think it and in the long run this is really what reality is, so far from the mind and mirror of man, who cannot even conceive of it." (*Verve*)

This ultimate material reality which he defines in old age, is what he earlier named "surreality," and it is upon an approximation of this that he wove the network of his poetry. It is the field of mental perception and physical sensitivity wherein unapparent relationships are grasped between objects. Beyond these relationships lies the infinite, i.e. the realm at whose borders our faculties fail. But within the charmed circle of these relationships, imperceptible to the common breed and attained as if through a mystic chance by those who may call themselves poets for lack of a better word, the artist has the impression of real creativeness. Less optimistic than Saint-Pol-Roux, Reverdy concedes that it is an illusion, but it is the guiding force, nonetheless, of the artist's work and more satisfying to his mystic thirst than any cult.

The test of the quality of a being is then not the degree of inner (dream) or outer (rarefication) escape in which he engages, but the objects toward which he radiates and by which he is represented, or with which he is identified by the immediacy of the image. Otherwise, he is unthinkable, non-existent. In the deserts of non-existence there is no real art. By his penetration of the concrete, the quality and limits of the mind can be recognized and judged. Man's roots are in heaven but as a tree upturned, whose leaves touch the soil, it is this contact with the tangible that gives promises of illuminations.

Undisturbed by polemics, personal affiliations or schisms with colleagues—as is the case with the surrealists —Pierre Reverdy comes closer to defining the spiritual and aesthetic position of the modern poet than anyone else in France in his time. A more striking personality, Apollinaire left a more fragmental *poetics* and did not have the benefit of a long life span to give it consistency. But the test of the value is not in theory, it is in the poetry itself. Although Reverdy, in a cruel moment says of the critic: "When certain critics speak of poetry, it is a little as if veterinarians tried to treat human ills," nonetheless let us attempt to find in the poetry—to the degree of our receptivity—the elements which the poet in his prose statements indicated as his points of orientation.

Reverdy's first collected works suggested that very combination of heaven and earth which was to serve as the locale of his poetry: "Les épaves du ciel," heaven, the infinite, coupled with "débris," suggesting shipwreck, but very concrete and objective remains of the unthinkable infinite. Making his début in the literary world, significantly at a time of war, he considered death, rampant everywhere, not the mysterious intruder as in Maeterlinck's symbolist representations, but a common denominator of life, not a robber of life but its spouse.

Reverdy's universe is an immense blackboard on which part of the great design has been erased. The poet's intention seems to have been to focus his spotlights on the bits which remained here and there. He seemed not to care to guess at the connections. In fact the main distinction he later indicated between prose and poetry was not one of form. (There is really no need to draw a distinction between Reverdy's own poems in prose and poems in free verse.) The difference lies for him between juxtaposition and reasonable connection, the independence of parts in contrast to the succession of ideas. He is not an

architect but an interpreter of lines, the broken, disconnected lines of life, blocked sometimes by those of death.

Departure

The horizon bends
      the days are getting longer
        Voyage
A heart leaps in a cage
        A bird sings
        About to die
Another door will open

At the end of the hall
      where there is glowing
      a star
A dark woman
      The lantern of the train
      About to depart

[L'horizon s'incline
         Les jours sont plus longs
         Voyage
     Un coeur saute dans une cage
        Un oiseau chante
        Il va mourir
Une autre porte va s'ouvrir
        Au fond du couloir
         Où s'allume
         Une étoile
Une femme brune
      La lanterne du train qui part] [8]

The connections are lacking because often they are unknown to the poet himself. This undirected work, the
product of a divine chance, casts a charm over the shad-

ows which constitute life and which have no outlet from the compact walls of the earth.

His world of detached images is a depopulated world in his earliest poems—not incomprehensibly so since its basis is wartime, depleted Paris. It is a world constantly on the verge of stopping in its movement. One of the strangest sensations throughout Reverdy's poems is the constant awareness we have of the turning of the world, like a cardiac who is the more conscious of his heartbeat in the fear that it might stop at any moment. Indeed, several times the earth actually stops in its rotation at Reverdy's bidding as objects assume their infinite repose: "The world shuts up shop silently and all at once." [9] Many of these poems are, like Mallarmé's *Igitur,* the poet's sensation of death while still in life.

Sound of Bell

All is snuffed out
The wind passes singing
And the trees quiver
The animals are dead
Look
The stars have stopped shining
The earth no longer turns
A head bends
With hair sweeping away night
The last bell left standing
Strikes midnight

[Tout s'est éteint
Le vent passe en chantant
Et les arbres frissonnent

Les animaux sont morts
Il n'y a plus personne
                    Regarde
Les étoiles ont cessé de briller
                    La terre ne tourne plus
Une tête s'est inclinée
                    Les cheveux balayant la nuit
Le dernier clocher resté debout
                    Sonne minuit] [10]

Upon this earth constantly bordering on eternity, the simplest objects have a geometric infinity, and contain a dose of the eternal. As a result the poet walks in a forest not of familiar symbols as was the case for Baudelaire but where the familiar things like a tree, a bird, a flower, a roof are strange and outside of natural phenomena. Reverdy possessed, along with the surrealists, that new poetic eye which discerns the eternal in the concrete and is no longer satisfied to associate the infinite with the realm of abstractions. Reverdy achieves this "new measure between the hand and the eye" by a most unobtrusive yet exact technique.

First there is protraction and contraction. Walls are forever moving away, rooms stepping out of their dimensions, windows out of their frames, the horizon falling off or several appearing at the same time. A small detail of a perceived object suddenly looms immense, becomes more important than the whole and completely overthrows our concept of proportion or symmetry. Then, objects step out of line by the unexpectedness of their movement. It is "the perspective of chance." [11] Trees take weird positions, houses sway, a window draws away its pane, a wall moves back, a roof rises, a door bends, the earth bends. Or else, movement stops where one expected it: the pendulum stops, the stars stop in their heavenly course. Things start contradicting the laws of nature: flowers are black and leaves never green, and the sun sings with a sweet sound; color mingles with the sound.

It is evident that Reverdy was a contemporary of Chirico. Many of his verbal images are sister-visions of Chirico's solitary streets and arches and unfriendly windows. This is the obvious similarity. There is a more subtle one: the material effect of intangible force: "the sun swells at the tip of a stalk of colored waterfall."

Sun

Someone has just left
The room
Leaving behind a sigh
Deserted life
The street
And the open window
A ray of sun
On the green lawn

[Quelqu'un vient de partir
Dans la chambre
Il reste un soupir
La vie déserte
La rue
Et la fenêtre ouverte
Un rayon de soleil
Sur la pelouse verte] [12]

Or the effect of estrangement is produced by the negative verb used with a positive reality. The *tour de force* that can be achieved by a "ne—pas" or "autre."

A lamp that is not lit, the door that does not open, the house where one does not enter! The static tableaus that he enfolds before us are beyond the dimensions of space, and free from "the armor of time," and only touched by the sense of space that resides in his heart. Indeed, the use of the present tense gives an undetermined time measure.

At times the simplicity of his work is marred by a relapse into symbolist technique to which he himself is conscious of being drawn: the symmetrical, rational coupling of abstract with concrete. That is the source of the monotony which sets in sometimes in his poems. But when the coupling rises above the analogy and enters into the realm of reality then it enhances rather than lulls the vision. When synaesthesia is accepted at its face value, there is a veritable galaxy of images: silence falls heavily on the ground without breaking, hands ring, minutes sparkle at the tip of branches, the mountain whistles with its tail lost at the shores of the humid lashes of the sea. In "Ronde nocturne" he constructs a stairway to heaven:

On the horizon, without a sound, someone rises to heaven
The stairs creak
They are artificial
It is a parable or a passageway
The hour that's escaping flies with a single wing

[A l'horizon sans bruit quelqu'un montait au ciel
L'escalier craque

Il est artificiel
C'est une parabole ou une passerelle
L'heure qui s'échappait ne bat plus que d'une aile] [13]

There are symbols, but fortunately his symbols are not
too mysteriously significant, too philosophically contrived.
They are: a man, a house, a train, a woman's voice, a
room, a curtain, a tree, a bell, a flame. They have representative qualities, but they are concrete, there is vagueness
not in the symbols themselves but in their fortuitous encounter with each other. It is the triumph of the part over
the whole. The part is greater than the whole, for were
you to see the whole you would give it *limit*. But seeing
vividly that little patch of the whole, stripped of its usual
associations, you feel that its scope is boundless.

Nomad

The door which does not open
The hand which passes
Afar a glass which is breaking
The lamp smokes
The sparks which light up
The sky is blacker
Over the roofs
Sundry animals
Shadowless

A look
A dark speck
The house remaining unentered.

(La porte qui ne s'ouvre pas
La main qui passe
Au loin un verre qui se casse
La lampe fume

Les étincelles qui s'allument
        Le ciel est plus noir
             Sur les toits
Quelques animaux
Sans leur ombre
          Un regard
          Une tache sombre
La maison où l'on n'entre pas)[14]

Reverdy's world of detached visions falls "between two worlds," earthy but not earthbound: through it the poet wanders in solitary fashion, unwilling to compromise with nature's yardstick.

The lonely journey undertaken by those who have the power to discern chips of heaven in the bric à brac of earth makes of them giants among their fellowmen:

    Those who are a source of disdain
Those who hold within them the drop of eternity necessary
    to life
Those who have never known their limitations
Passing along the road with heaven alone as a roof bend their
    heads
The stars have got caught in their hair . . .

    [Ceux qui sont une source de mépris
Ceux qui portent en eux la goutte d'éternité nécessaire a la vie
    Ceux qui n'ont jamais connu leur mesure
      En passant sur la route qui n'est recouverte que par le
        ciel baissent la tête
      Des étoiles sont restées prises dans leurs cheveux][15]

It is the simplest words of the language which convey his eternity:

Everything would frighten in the midst of this world
    In the world
        where music has another tune
      The measured steps another number
      And glass another reflection

[Tour ferait peur au milieu de ce monde
    dans le monde
        où la musique a un autre air
      les pas comptés un autre nombre
      Et la glace un autre reflet] [16]

Finally the frontiers are passed: "The roots of earth hang out beyond the limits of earth." ("The Red Head," *La Plupart du temps*.)

The final lap of the journey is less stoical, the anguish more insistent, though still succinct. As in the case of André Breton, Eluard, and Aragon, the stress of World War II temporarily arrests the mystical anguish by the overwhelming proportions of the physical and human catastrophe it unleashes. In "Le Chant des morts" (The Song of the Dead) though the technique is the same, the images are not those of a transformed world but of a mutilated one.

Motionless and too real in matter
Nothing.

His own inner abyss becomes harder to endure, the image of death masks at times the presence of eternity as it did not do during World War I.

This then is the work of unobtrusive Pierre Reverdy who has witnessed three generations of literary coteries, who has survived two wars, emerging neither as a heroic war bard, nor as a spectacular figure, but walking quietly in the margin of world events, in the margin of poetic revolution. However, he has produced a poetry which is far from marginal. With the simplest words in the French language, the universal words and the earthy ones, and some of the translucent ones interspersed, he has labeled the most common forms and beings with a mystic significance not because he spurns the world as it is, but to leave on it the imprint of his love of life. For life is to him not the antithesis of death, not a passage, but an absolute condition.

N O T E S

1. *Le Livre de mon bord* (1930-36), Mercure de France, Paris, 1948, p. 151.

2. *Ibid.,* p. 36.

3. p. 74.

4. p. 72.

5. p. 53.

6. p. 12.

7. p. 114.

8. "Départ," *La Plupart du temps* (1915-1922), NRF, Gallimard, Paris, 1945, p. 165.

9. "Au Cercle qui ferme les yeux," *Main d'oeuvre* (1913-49), Mercure de France, Paris, 1949, p. 197.

10. "Son de Cloche," *La Plupart du temps,* p. 170.

11. "Mille Murmures dans le rang," *Main d'oeuvre,* p. 83.

12. "Soleil," *La Plupart du temps,* p. 186.

13. From "Ronde nocturne," *La Plupart du temps,* p. 168.

14. "Nomade," *Ibid.,* p. 181.

15. From "Les Jockeys camouflés," *Ibid.,* p. 240.

16. From "Le Reflet dans la glace," *La Plupart du temps,* p. 334.

the road

◑

breton and the surrealist mind—

the influences of

freud and hegel

Surrealism, like the legendary phoenix, was born of death and ashes. The group of young writers and artists who chose to be linked under this banner participated in the burning and the funeral of an ideology which they had embraced only a few years earlier and were quickly abandoning as futile and futureless.

The demise of Dada in 1924 is generally passed over humorously or indulgently, or even anecdotally, in the

annals of literary history. But as the years go by and the
literary currents take on their consequential perspectives,
the act of rejection involved in the funeral of Dadaism
takes on added significance.

Dada had been an acute state of protest against society,
literature, and those ideologies which had contributed to
the destruction and chaos of World War I. The rebels
were young men, who came to Paris from all over the
world, and attributed the political failures to ineffective
thinking. They attacked *logic,* which had proved a tragic
basis for action. They attacked by the same token the artist
who had fled into his ivory tower and let the world
crumble around him.

The Dadaists summarized their sense of futility by the
word "rien." They endured their nihilism not with tears
but with a mocking smirk, a shameless disdain of the
reality which embraced them and which appeared so
wanting. All the exhibitionism and anti-social vindictives
associated with Dadaism were motivated by this concerted
protest of the moment.

But the moment passed, and the Dadaists realized that
the futility of Dada was even greater than the futility of
the reality against which it protested. From then on the
attitude of revolt ceased and the concerted efforts were
directed toward means of surmounting the initial nihilism. It dawned on these young writers and artists that perhaps it was not man's mind that was wanting, nor even
the world of realities that was absurd, but the limited
utilization of the mind and of the objects of its experience.
Before becoming an art, surrealism became a philosophy

and a way of life. The Dadaists, transforming themselves into surrealists under the leadership of André Breton, sought a philosophical foundation for their art. Nietzsche, who had proved so popular at the dawn of the century, seemed to them too destructive and egocentric in his notion of reality; Kierkegaard's anguish was too passive to give an impetus to new thought. What the surrealists needed was supporting evidence for their dream-wish that something more resourceful than logic might be found to endow life with fuller significance, and that the objects of thought might have a more elastic reality. Their adamant desire to transform this absurd, unappetizing world had a deeply metaphysical motivation. But since they wanted outlet for their mysticism without recourse to religion, the transcendence had to occur *hic et nunc*. The purpose of their existence and art, then, was to seek both physical and metaphysical satisfaction by pushing back the frontiers of logical reality and revealing the infinite possibilities within the scope of the concrete world. This process implied a closer association between the one who sees and the object of his sight. The venture was an act of creation and an expression of vertiginous freedom on the part of the artist. To Breton it meant a deeper, more passionate consciousness of the sensory world. Eluard saw it as a loosening of the horizon's belt through an increased fertility of the senses, the abandonment of accepted perspectives and the cultivation of prescience. For Louis Aragon it meant the discovery of "the face of the infinite in the concrete forms" discerned along the paths of earth.

In re-examining the age-old concepts of reality and in attempting to break down the antithesis between matter and mind, which had been accepted for so long, surrealists found support in Hegel; and in searching for a basis for the faith they had that the mind's scope could outreach its determined logical powers, they looked into the investigations that Freud had made into the unconscious. The initial emphasis on psychic automatism and enthusiasm for dream revelations in surrealist writings point to Freud as the earlier of the two Germanic influences.

It was while he was a student of psychiatry, before World War I, that André Breton, the future leader of the surrealist movement, first came in contact with Freud's studies. In 1916 while an intern at the neurological center in Nantes, he had occasion to practice psychiatry and psychotherapy on the wounded. In 1919, while still preoccupied with Freud, he was beginning to turn his interests from medicine to literature; psychoanalysis proved a convenient bridge for him between the scientific attitude of objective investigation and a literary mind's philosophical introspection. Freud granted the young poetmedico an interview in Vienna in 1921 in answer to a letter from Breton, which he called "the most touching that I have ever received." [1] Breton found the greatest psychiatrist of our time, as he considered Freud, very reticent, except for his obvious dislike of France, which had remained the only country indifferent to his work. Indeed Freud was translated into French much later than into English; *Der Witz und seine Beziehung zum Unbewussten,* published in 1905, translated into English in 1917, did not appear in French until 1930, as one surrealist writer deploringly points out.[2] In sharp contrast with this general lack of interest on the part of the French, Breton and his *confrères* gave plenty of publicity to Freud and to his discoveries, in their two major periodicals, *La Révolution Surréaliste* and *Le Surréalisme au Service de la Révolution* (1924-33). In his very first manifesto, dated 1924, Breton gave Freud ample credit for his discoveries in dream interpretation, his method of investigation and the new rights he thereby granted to the human imagination. Breton's knowledge of the history of psychology made it possible for him to judge the originality of Freud's work and to name in a most scholarly manner all his predecessors; he was indiscreet enough to suggest a correction to Freud's bibliography of *The Interpretation of Dreams,* much to the embarrassment of the author. He foresaw as the ultimate achievement of dream study the marriage of the two states, in appearance so contradictory, of dream and reality, into one sort of absolute reality which he called surreality.

The simplest and most obvious influence of Freudian psychology can be found in the accounts of dreams written by practically everyone of the fifty or so *bona fide* surrealists, who contributed to the surrealist periodicals. Both writers and artists, more in the spirit of experimentation and investigation than of pure creative expression, participated in the activity of relating or writing dreams, and with as much candor and even less inhibition than Freud, interpreted their dreams. Robert Desnos, the most remarkable of these dreamers,[3] could fall into a state of dreaming at the least provocation and as a result produced a rich flow of verbal images for the admiring colleagues present. There were various categories of dreams: the natural dream, the prophetic dream, and most often the self-induced one, such as the flamboyant, libido-ridden dreams of Dali. There were "experimental" dreams, such as Tristan Tzara's "Grains et issues" in which "the hands have been pulled out of all the clocks in the world" and we see a population hungrily awaiting "the most extravagant innovations." [4] In the analytical commentary which accompanies the part-prose, part-verse transcription of the dream, Tzara states that when the dream becomes accepted as a complementary rather than contrasting experience to the waking part of life, our notions and feelings will be transformed to such an extent that the rules which govern our actions now will become as inapplicable as Euclidian geometry is to the widened range of today's universe. The dream, for him, transforms phenomena, by facilitating the synthesis which is the basis of poetic knowledge.

In *Les Vases Communicants,* dedicated to Freud, André Breton envisaged existence as a composite of two urns, the dream and the state of wakefulness, constantly connected with each other and contributing to each other's intensity. He noted not only the added keenness of the mind but the greater rapidity of thought in the dream. In observing the effect of the dream on imagery he found the same type of displacement of objects and things, and verbal condensations in the poet's dream thought as Freud had observed in his clinical cases as well as in his own dreams. In this work Breton gave Freud credit for having been the first to pronounce himself on the question: "What happens to time, space and the principle of causality in dreams." [5] Sending him a copy of the book, he paid tribute to Freud's "keen and marvelous sensitivity," and stated that the purpose of his book was to show on what roads of psychological conquest Freud had directed the surrealists.

Verbal expression linking the visions of the dream state with conscious perceptions is also the core of one of the most original of Paul Eluard's works, *Les Dessous d'une vie ou la Pyramide humaine,* wherein the poet envisions human experiences in the form of a pyramid, the narrow peak of which is the limited range of the lucid state, and the broad base the receptivity of the full, solid subterranean strata of the subconscious, the dream where all his desires are born, where receptivity is keener than the sense perceptions of his waking hours. He can hear the language of the deaf and dumb and with the "pure faculty of sight" can envisage such images as "perpendicular green" upon which he picks "raspberries white as milk."

Another aspect of Freudian influence was the practice of automatic writing, which was considered a safer road toward the subconscious mind than the interpretation of dreams. This process became for the surrealists a form of self-administered psychoanalysis: placing themselves in a state of stupefying attentiveness they tried to shut out all outside disturbances and to give free play to the inner powers of association of words and the images which these suggested. Most of what they called "Textes surréalistes" is fundamentally automatic writing. Those of Paul Eluard and Tristan Tzara are particularly fecund in uncanny imagery. In his *Genèse et perspective artistique du surréalisme,* Breton stressed automatic thinking as the common basis of surrealist poetry and art, and declared it to be the sole mode of expression fully satisfactory to the eye and ear, for the rhythmic unity which it produced corresponded "to the nondistinction more and more established of the functioning of the senses and of the intellect." He categorically claimed that a work cannot be called surrealist unless it embraced the entire psychophysical field.

A third form of Freudian experimentation was the intentional simulation of states of mental abnormality. The "Fol" of Saint-Pol-Roux became a more important character of poetry. *L'Immaculée Conception* was a collaboration between Breton and Eluard which set out: "to prove that the mind, poetically conditioned, is in a normal man capable of reproducing in their broad lines the most paradoxical and eccentric verbal manifestations . . . without risk of lasting trouble, and without compromising its faculty of equilibrium." [6] In this work the writers set themselves a triple aim: to imitate delirium, artificially assume the various forms of insanity, and thus establish a method of investigating the widest range of mental activity. The most constant exploitation of this vein has been Salvadore Dali's paranoiac paintings.

These exercises in uninhibited, and sometimes erotic, writing and exploration of sensations beyond the control of reason were to sharpen, to renovate poetic imagery, and to incorporate into the poet's technique Freud's observations on the role of language in dream and dream interpretation: the condensation that results in a density of imagagery; displacement of the senses of time and space in the vision; the importance of figurative language. Freud had noted, and the surrealists have actually illustrated in their poems, that concrete terms owing to the evolution of their connotation and to their subsequent mutation of role, produce more frequent and more rapid mental associations than do conceptual ones: consider the many disturbing uses to which elementary words like "table," "homme," "sable," have been put in surrealist imagery, or provocative ones like "épave," "miroir," "sein," "pyramide," "reverbère" etc. which are often the kernel of the surrealist image and play central roles similar to the clocks, stairs, platters and umbrellas of surrealist paintings. Incorrect meaning attributed to words, which Freud explains as the simultaneous expression of more than one dream-thought, due to psychic disturbance in the subject, are ever dominant in surrealist writing. However, herein lies a major difference between Freud and the surrealists, for the latter do not consider these misuses as indications of frustrations but rather of the richness and versatility of the poet's imagination. Finally, the strong element of absurdity common in dreams, and a certain type of unsought humor revealed in the hallucinations of the deranged mind were intentionally practiced in surrealist writing to demonstrate a super-sense of reality.

The surrealists' tributes to Freud continued to the end of the psychologist's life. When Freud was rumored to be

imprisoned by the Nazis in 1938, Breton wrote an indignant letter in a London periodical, in which he declared
that Freud had been "a life of inspiration which we hold
as dear to us as our own," [7] that in his attempts to seek
"human emancipation in the widest sense" he had been
the reincarnation of Goethe; he designated Freud as "he
from whom so many of us derive our finest reason for existence and action."

Here are strong words of praise; but despite their adherence to Freud the surrealists did not find him as re-
sponsive to their work as they had been to his. Upon receiving Breton's *Les Vases communicants* he had had to
confess in his letter to the author that it was not at all
clear to him what surrealism was. "Perhaps I am not
made to understand it, he said, for I am so far removed
from art." [8] The reason he could not understand it was
that the surrealists were launched on a much more adventurous investigation than he; theirs was not an observation
or interpretation of the subconscious world but a coloni-
zation. In spite of their admiration of Freud, the poets
observed shortcomings not in the psychologist's *method*
but in its application and conclusions. They felt that
Freud had been too reticent in his interpretation of
dreams; they deplored the fact that he denied the existence of the prophetic dream. The dream as a clinical interpretation of the disintegration of personality—with
which Freud had been exclusively concerned—was one
thing, but as a form of literature and art it could not be
justified unless it also revealed the *unification* of the personality of the artist: his adjustment to two planes of real-

ity, no longer visualized as contradictory. This had been suggested by Freud, but unintentionally: he had, says Breton, "without knowing it found . . . in the dream the principle of the conciliation of opposites." [9] The greatest weakness seen in Freud was precisely the fact that he drew too definite a barrier between the exterior world and the dream experience. It was not sufficient to show the effect of conscious experience on the dream; the surrealists wanted to go one step further and show the effect of the dream state on consciousness. Breton justifies the poet's stepping ahead of the psychologist master by a quotation from Freud himself:

"Poets are in the knowledge of the soul our masters, for they drink at sources not yet made accessible to science. Why has the poet not expressed himself more precisely on the nature of the dream?" [10]

The interpretation of dreams, psychoanalysis, the study of the irrationalities of the insane, utilized as methods of explaining quirks and frustrations of neurotics, were inconsequential to the surrealists. Breton derides the fact that psychologists would interpret the surrealist Yves Tanguy's paintings on the basis of childhood sin obsessions. As he states in his *Second Manifesto:* "it is not surprising to observe that as surrealism progresses, it applies its attention to something other than the solution of a psychological problem no matter how interesting it may be." A point was reached in the thinking of the surrealists where Freud could not accompany them. It was "désolant," as Breton pointed out in his "Réserves quant à la signification historique des investigations sur le rêve," that although an alleged monist, Freud had said: "psychic reality is a particular form of existence which must not be confused with material reality." [11]

On the contrary, Freud's methods had pointed the way to that substratum of consciousness wherein the distinction between the sensory and the intellectual functioning of the mind is erased, and thereby the disparity between the sensory evidence of the outer world and the psychic reality experienced by the mind yields in favor of their inherent unity. Consequently, the greater freedom of mental activity which Freud's methods made possible was not to be enjoyed as a means of *escape* from exterior reality but for better knowledge of the world of matter. Breton deplores man's nightly exile from consciousness and the neglect of this potential reservoir of life and thought. The dreamlife should not be considered subservient to the wakeful state, used merely to interpret and clarify consciousness. Man had an actual *need* for the dream experience, and the sharper his mystic or artistic sensitivities were, the more he needed the dream experience. What Freud took in dream interpretation for symbols of the conscious life, Breton and his colleagues wanted to grasp as naked realities, significant and even downright essential to the better and more complete knowledge of existence. Man had essayed "interpretation" of the world for so long a period; was it not time at last to pass to the more adventurous and fruitful task of *transforming* it? The forces of the mind that produced the state of the dream could if properly utilized give a much needed encouragement to the effort of transfiguration.

This was not an evasion of reality, nor a release of the spirit from its earthly bonds, but an *expansion,* an enrichment of human existence. What the surrealists were basically doing was revising through the study of the dream their notion of reality. It is at this point in the development of their thought that Hegel lent them support.

The surrealists' appreciation of German literature, their companionship with several German colleagues, principally the artist Max Ernst, as well as a defiant attitude toward the existing political post-war regime in France, made them inclined to become germanophiles during the 1920's and in the early pre-Hitler 1930's. They reintroduced to the French public a wealth of German literature, the most striking example of which was a luxurious and powerfully illustrated new edition of Achim von Arnim's *Contes bizarres*[12] (the nineteenth-century translation by Théophile Gautier fils). In interpreting one of his own dreams, Breton speaks of his subconscious longing for understanding between France and "the marvelous country of thought and light which in one century gave birth to Kant, Hegel, Feuerbach and Marx." [13] As late as 1935 in one of their general manifestoes the surrealists declared "hopelessly *chauvine*" Julian Benda's demand for reparations and his disinclination to forgive the Germans.[14] In that same year when Breton was asked in an interview what he thought of the intellectual state of things in Germany, he asserted, despite his great antipathy for

Hitler's regime, that the surrealists' confidence in German
thought had not been shaken, that they considered it the
most pertinent to contemporary civilization, and that they
had faith in the uninterrupted cultural lineage proceeding from Hegel to Engels. He stated that the surrealists
considered themselves recipients of that heritage, which
in their opinion should not be called German but Euro-
pean; and in defining their position toward German philosophy Breton made the subtle distinction of calling it
not "German philosophy," but "in the German language."

The only mention of Hegel in the *First Manifesto* had
been an inconsequential one within a quotation from
Gérard de Nerval. But by the 1930's when the surrealists
considered themselves within the throes of an intellectual
and moral "crise de conscience," it was the consensus of
opinion that Hegel had become the pillar of their thinking. In his *Second Manifesto* Breton declared that the
Hegelian concept of the penetration of the exterior world
into subjective existence had remained uncontested. In his
"Qu'est-ce que le surréalisme?" he pointed out that the
influence of Hegel was most felt as the surrealists realized
that they were concerned with the long-range problem of
knowledge as well as the immediate one of expression.
In a pertinent article on the notebook kept by Lenin of
Hegel's principal concepts, André Thinion called attention to the fact that in 1932 when he and his colleagues
were taking such an active interest in Hegel and published
in French for the first time fragments of the Hegel-Lenin
dialogue, Hegel's *Science of Logic* had not yet been translated into French. In his introduction to the Lenin notes,

published in *Le Surréalisme au Service de la Révolution,*
Thinion asserted that in France the surrealists "with the
exception of a few professional philosophers, are alone in
claiming derivation from Hegelian thought and in referring constantly their activities to this ideology." [15] He states
that these ideas are of the highest importance to the surrealists and have had the power of shock on them, have
led them to grasp the evolution of material and intellectual existence.

Which were these thoughts that Lenin had underlined
and which clarified the surrealists' notion of the human
world? It was Hegel's stress on the superiority of the concrete over the abstract, his belief in the inner unity of contradictory conditions or phenomena, and particularly his
definition of knowledge as the linking of thought with its
object. The surrealists inferred from Hegel that the true
understanding of existence depended on the knowledge
of the interrelation of the subjective and the objective,
which in turn meant a refusal of the kind of idealism that
sought something finer than the concrete manifestations
of reality. The metaphysical experience then, could be
reached not through transcendence but through a successful tuning of mind with matter. As Tristan Tzara said, "it
amounts to the conciliation of man in the making with
the reality of the exterior world." [16]

This was indeed the objective of Breton and Louis
Aragon in *Nadja* and *Le Paysan de Paris* respectively. In
trying to blend his coherent perceptions with the irrational
one of Nadja, a lovely but insane young woman, Breton
aimed at what he considered a superior existence, in

which the contradictions caused by the nonparallel vision between Nadja and himself would be overcome purely by the effort of the mind and the acuteness of perceptions. For after all, says Breton, relying on a quotation from Hegel, the test of one individual's superiority over another is not in the search for existence on a superior sphere but in the power to express better than someone else this self-same world. In *Le Paysan de Paris* Aragon sought the marvels of daily chance meetings and chance events which transformed ordinary living. The unexpected disorder in physical and social laws, which caused this chance meeting of objects, persons and situations, was the only satisfying human knowledge of the infinite, for to grasp the concrete forms of disorder was the outer limit of the mental faculty. In both these works dealing with philosophical search for the absolute the measuring stick is knowledge of the concrete forms and objects, and the mind's elasticity in transforming them.

This return from purely abstract thinking to a need for understanding of the concrete was what another surrealist, René Crevel, called the possibility of man's acting upon his universe. In this universe it is the object that seized anew the eye of the poet and the painter. According to Paul Eluard's definition of the poetic activity, it consisted in inventing objects by deviating from their admitted physical properties and accepted roles, and thereby changing the world. Breton called this process a crisis of the object in his *Le Surréalisme et la peinture* and gave Hegel due credit for his part in the upheaval; for in this deviation from the natural object the surrealists were avoiding one of the dangers pointed out by Hegel in his *Aesthetics:* the servile imitation of nature and its limit-setting properties. It is not only in the deviation of the object but in the relative position of the subject and the object that Hegel serves as guide. Breton notes in a more recent writing (in the preface of his *Anthology of Black Humor*), that in indicating this very difference in perspective Hegel succeeded in pointing out the true difference between romanticism and modernism: the romantic draws the object within himself and makes an abstraction of it, while the true modern projects himself into the concrete existence of the object.

Hegel's imprint can also be noted in the philosophical significance attributed by the surrealists to the creation of the metaphor. For them it is not a mere form of speech but the crystallization of concept. The power of their thinking, the profoundness of their emotional experience is judged by the originality and density of the metaphor. Even as Hegel had deemed the genius of metaphorical diction to be a test of the potency of the mind and a rejection of simple reality, the successful metaphor becomes in surrealist writing, as we shall see, the measure not merely of literary satisfaction but a victory over ordinary existence.

Finally Hegel's disdain of the prosaic mind is cited in support of a similar attitude shared by the surrealists. They consider the poetic art almost a priesthood and as the epitome of human creativeness, as in fact Hegel called it the universal art and the one best capable of representing the successive positions of life.

It might appear that the two influences pointed out here were in opposing directions: one toward greater subjectivity, the other toward a keener comprehension of the object of man's awareness. Yet there is a basic affinity in the kind of impact they had. Faced with a world of paradoxes, the surrealists were primarily seeking an answer to their longing for innate unity among the contradictions; they tried to satisfy their passion for complete contact with the world and their desire to apply to its representation the inner resources of intuitive intelligence, which René Crevel so aptly called: *L'Esprit contre la raison.* Both Hegel and Freud indicated a path of freedom: liberation from exaggerated abstraction on the one hand, deliverance from excessive lucidity on the other.

But the surrealists could not subscribe totally to the system of Hegel any more than they could wholly adhere to Freud. The failing discovered in the case of Hegel was "the idealist error," i.e., Hegel had considered real things to be a degree of realization of the absolute idea; whereas in Breton's understanding of the word and in the poetic and artistic interpretation given to it by the surrealists, the ideal is not an independent concept but the result of man's mental transposition and translation of the material universe.

Thus, both Freud and Hegel proved to be influences in the most salutary sense of the word: they pointed a direction but raised an objection strong enough to lead to subsequent originality on the part of their disciples. As can be observed by examining these two influences, one of the basic characteristics of the surrealist mind is its uncompromising will to find a foolproof unity in the universe. Through contingency with Freud and Hegel the surrealists were able to outgrow their initial nihilism and advance a credo of hope, based on faith in the potential capacity of the human mind for synthesis, synthesis of the human dream and material reality. In both philosophical outlooks, so contradictory on the surface, the surrealists found ground for the fundamental support they were seeking, reassurance for their monistic philosophy. As Crevel spoke of Hegel: "Knowledge is the eternal and infinite rapprochemont of thought with its object." [17] He saw in Hegel the weapon with which to fight the narcissism of those who incorporate the world into their own meager, mediocre anguish, thereby obliterating it.

"The narcissistic individual, the one who has remained in the expressive stage has eaten up the universe and because he has devoured it, suppressed the objects, becomes himself the object, and thereby not only becomes insufficient unto himself but destroys himself. In the island whose outline is that of his little person this isolated being succumbs before the mirror he has questioned—he has questioned the most mediocre, the most vain, the most superficial of waters."

In his "Psycho-dialectique" Crevel continues by pondering the exact contribution of Freud. He has thrown light upon the unknown recesses of the subconscious and measured it against consciousness. But what is to be the result? Is he just accentuating the antithesis? When will the synthesis take place? Psychological dualism only produces questions. If the brilliant experiments of Freud merely encourage this "inquietude," he will have contributed to a futile "psycho-dialectic," said Crevel.

Likewise, for Breton dream experiment is valid only as a means of proceeding from the abstract to the concrete, from the subject to the object, which, he says, is the sole road to knowledge. The findings of Freud, then, must serve to solidify the Hegelian philosophy of reality with its emphasis on the concrete. The constant shuttling between the subject and the object, which Crevel deplored, would be replaced by a permanent integral connection cementing abstract and concrete reality into a single framework of dream-wakefulness. That is the poetic and artistic task that the surrealists set themselves.

Considered in this light surrealism was a twentieth-century integration of art and philosophy. Believing their efforts to run parallel to those of the modern scientists, they have tried to give proof that the arts are not behind the sciences in man's progress toward knowledge. Theirs was a gallant endeavor to surmount the superficial absurdity of life. We shall note in what follows, their concrete achievements in literary language and pictorial representation.

N O T E S

1. André Breton, "Interview du Professor Freud", *Les Pas perdus*, Paris, 1924, p. 118.

2. Jean Frais-Wittman, "Le Mot d'esprit et ses rapports avec l'inconscient," *Le Surréalisme au Service de la Révolution*, Vol. II, p. 28.

3. For a while Desnos went regularly to Breton's apartment and fell asleep right after dinner, making ecstatic pronouncements upon

awaking. His sleeping séances became more and more deep and complicated until one night Breton had to fetch a doctor to wake Desnos.

4. Tristan Tzara, *"Grains et issues"*, *Le Surréalisme au Service de la Révolution*, Vol. VI, p. 56.

5. Breton, *Les Vases communicants*, Cahiers libres, Paris, 1932, p. 16.

6. Breton and Eluard, *L'Immaculée Conception*, Editions surréalistes, Paris, 1930, p. 28.

7. Breton, "Freud at Vienna", *London Bulletin*, London 1938, no. 2, p. 2.

8. Breton-Freud, Correspondance, *Le Surréalisme au Service de la Révolution*, Vol. V, p. 11.

9. Breton, "Réserves quant à la signification historique des investigations sur le rêve", *Ibid.*, Vol. IV, p. 9.

10. Breton, *Les Vases communicants*, p. 163.

11. *Ibid.*

12. The German literary influences are discussed in my book, *Literary Origins of Surrealism*.

13. See "Du Temps que les surréalistes avaient raison," *Documents surréalistes* (Paris, ed. by Nadeau) Aux Editions du Seuil, 1948, p. 311.

14. *Ibid.*, p. 51.

15. A. Thinion, "En Lisant Hegel", *Le Surréalisme au Service de la Révolution*, Vol. III, p. 1.

16. Tristan Tzara, "Présentation d'une exposition de papiers collés de Picasso," *Documents surréalistes*, p. 277.

17. René Crevel, "Résumé d'une conférence," *Le Surréalisme etc.*, no. III, p. 35-6.

S   E   V   E   N

◑

the surrealist image

In his first manifesto, published in 1924, André Breton, who has maintained a pontifical position in the surrealist movement, declared that surrealism was a new mode of expression, which he and his colleagues had discovered and wished to put at the disposal of others. When the following year he took over the direction of the periodical, *La Révolution Surréaliste,* he stated that the principal aim of its founders was to raise the French language from the abject insignificance and stagnation to which it had been reduced under the influence of successful but mediocre authors like Anatole France. Five years later, in his second manifesto, he once more contended that the chief activity of surrealism was in the field of verbal reconstruction, and that social and political questions were of secondary concern. In *Entretiens* (1952), considering surrealist activities in retrospect, Breton again asserted that their purpose was "essentially and before all else" to put language in "a state of effervescence."

Now linguistic innovations are an essential function of the *ars poetica,* whether we look back on the enrichments of vocabulary achieved by the Renaissance poets, the discriminate choice of words of the classicists, the emotional flexibility of language discovered by the romanticists, or the elasticity of connotation cultivated by the symbolists. As Shelley pointed out in his *Defense of Poetry,* the poet, through his use of language, establishes the analogies among life's realities, but every so often when these associations have grown stale and lost their power of conveying integral thought, it is up to him to refresh his imagery and thereby preserve the vitality of language.

Breton, together with Louis Aragon, Paul Eluard, Tristan Tzara and some fifty other poets and artists, well versed in the history of literature, aesthetics and philosophy, and possessed of a very strong capacity for convictions, felt that they had arrived at a crucial moment in the development of the French language. They considered literature at an *impasse* and called the manner of writing of their elders degrading and cowardly. But instead of confining themselves to a local renovation of the poetic form, they welcomed all poets of any nationality who wished to participate in their systematic cult of the latent possibilities of language. They believed that their linguistic revolution could not only revive literature but lead to a new understanding of the objects designated by language and thereby situate them at the center of a new *mystique*.

A number of works are available which mark a consensus of opinion and establish the bases of surrealist composition: Breton's two manifestoes, Aragon's *Traité du style,* and a series of articles to be found in the annals of *La Révolution Surréaliste* (1924-29) and *Le Surréalisme au Service de la Révolution* (1931-33), among them the significant "Essai sur la situation de la poésie" by Tristan Tzara.

The creative role of language was strongly stressed in the surrealists' concept of poetry. Poetry was no longer to be an expression of ideas or emotions but the creation of a series of images, which would not necessarily owe their existence to an *a priori* subject. "Images think for me," said Paul Eluard in "Défense de savoir." And Aragon explained in the *Traité du style:* "In our time there are no longer any ideas; they are as rare as smallpox, but it goes without saying that there are images caught, and for once well caught, real slaps in the face of any kind of good sense." [1] Breton called ideas vain and ineffective compared to the force of the sudden, unexpected image. In his famous article, "Misère de la poésie," he tried to come to the rescue of Aragon, accused of subversion in his poem, "Front Rouge." But as far as its aesthetic value was concerned, he dismissed the controversial poem as being a hundred years behind the times despite its so-called modern subject. The fact that it had a definite subject matter to develop belied the contemporary state of poetic evolution, which according to Breton banishes unity of subject matter from the poem. It is Breton's belief that the speed of thinking is not superior to that of linguistic expression, which, therefore, should not be subservient to logical thought. Words brought together by creative intuition could explode in a dynamic image which would be more provocative than are abortive thoughts seeking words to give them a countenance,[2] he explains in his second manifesto. Images, then, are not to be *directed* by thoughts but should be conducive to them, and the function of the poem in regard to the reader is what Eluard called "donner à voir," *to give sight.* It is up to the reader to participate in the creative act of the author by deriving from his own pool of personal associations his particular stream of thought. And in order to allow the reader freedom of mental association there must be a compression of language and a minimum denominator of self-evident meaning.

Now the surrealists did not have in mind the type of imagery put into the French language by Verlaine and Mallarmé, i.e. terminology abstract in meaning and so undefined in connotation that it suggests moods rather than visions. On the contrary, their vocabulary is concrete in shape and color, in texture and intent, sometimes so precise as to be exclusive in use and technical in meaning. The words serving as stimuli or irritants to the senses were to produce their own images. Language was to be endowed with a benzedrine-like quality, and if expertly used, could grant pleasures beyond those induced by narcotics. Breton compares the spontaneity with which these images offer themselves and their habit-forming character to the stupefying state of mind produced by artifical paradises. In this state of subconscious stimulation the poet is alerted to the sensations that words can produce much in the manner that the painter is attracted to objects, which mean a different thing to each artist and speak a different language to each spectator. The surrealist poet in his use of words was approaching the painter's technique, and that is how a closer bond was established between poetry and art than ever before, and a greater gap between poetry and the literary forms that continued to have as their aim the expression of ideas.

A serious study of the quality and range of words was then, the *sine qua non* of poetry. As we have seen, a generation before the surrealists, Guillaume Apollinaire had envisaged the possibility of experiments and investigations in this field. Breton and his colleagues went so far as to establish a Central Bureau of Surrealist Research to experiment with writing and to accept communications relative to their research from outside their ranks. In a chapter of *Les Pas perdus,* characteristically called "Words without Wrinkles," Breton stated that the greatest poetic act was the understanding of the full destiny of words. He suggested ways of doing this: by studying the words themselves, the reaction of words to each other, the appearance of words and the effect of the figurative meaning on the

literal. To such considerations could be attributed provocative surrealist titles as "Le Revolver à cheveux blancs,"
(The Whitehaired Revolver), "Clair de terre," (Earth-
shine), "Les Yeux fertiles," (Fertile Eyes), "L'Homme
approximatif," (Approximative man), "Le Poisson soluble," (Soluble Fish), "Le Paysan de Paris," (The Peasant
of Paris).

Breton explained that it took him six months to write
his poem, "Forêt-noire," (of which the actual word count
is *thirty*), for he virtually "coddled" the words to determine the space they permitted between each other, their
tangency with innumerable other words which would not
appear in the poem, but with which the written words
came in contact in the author's mind during the process
of composition. The most evident if somewhat playful
demonstration of the spontaneous suggestive power of
words was the glossary composed by the surrealist poet,
Michel Leiris, which consisted of basic words and the images they evoke, as for example: "humain—la main hu-
mide, moite. L'as-tu connue, cette main? ingénu—le génie
nu; langage—bagage lent de l'esprit; révolution—solution de tout rêve; rumeur—brume des bruits qui meurent
au fond des rues; suicide—idée sûre de sursis." [3]

The poet's tolerance to words had to be increased; he
could help himself by dismissing the wrong words from
his mind. Which are the wrong words? Those that have
wandered too far afield from their concrete specifications,
those that have served too often to form rhymes, those
that have received the tag "poetic" through excessive
usage in poetry. Abused words can gain a new value if

their primitive meaning is sought out. Sometimes it is even advisable to give a word the wrong meaning, for words do not really tell a lie, and if they come to the poet's mind at a given moment it is because they fulfill a poetic necessity. Breton discovered that he sometimes unwittingly used a word whose true meaning he had forgotten; looking it up later he would find that his use of the word was not etymologically incorrect.

For a more drastic interpretation of the meaning of words we can refer to Aragon's *Traité du style,* in which he claims that dictionaries do not cover the full connotation of words; there is meaning contained in each syllable, according to him, and inherent in the very spelling of the words. Words are what another surrealist, Arpad Mezei, called "multidimensional," [4] in an evaluation of surrealist accomplishments in *Le Surréalisme en 1947* (Edition Pierre à Feu). Etymology, which is only one of its dimensions, has unfortunately been overstressed and has become its dead weight, according to Breton. Michel Leiris considers it a perfectly useless science; the poet must look for the secret ramifications of words in the entire domain of language, the canals created by the association of sounds, of forms and ideas. When this inner working of words is understood, language becomes prophetic and supplies a thread with which to guide us in the labyrinth of the mind, he explained in connection with his "Glossary."

To discover, then, what one might call the high voltage of words was to be the key to surrealist poetry. But in the composition of the poem, what is even more important than the right word is the happy marriage of words into illuminating (not elucidating) associations, which become the basis of the image. The surrealists found in automatic writing a rich hunting ground for the capture of word associations. It assumed the same importance in the technical equipment of the surrealist as the practice of scales to the musician. In this quasi-hypnotic state the hand writes or draws (for the same thing can be done in art) almost alone, and the pen or pencil transcribes spontaneously the subconscious affiliations we feel between the words. These "Surrealist texts," as they are called, must not be taken for poems. They are just a means of developing or enriching poetic consciousness; they also break down traditional word associations which are too deep-set to be warded off consciously, and which are not only ineffective in imagery but even detrimental to the component words involved in the tedious alliance. Words should be drawn together not by emotional kinship but by what Baudelaire called "sorcellerie évocatoire," (incantatory bewitchment) or in the more recent terminology of Aragon, "puissance incantatorie," (power of incantation). Sometimes it is nothing more than assonance or alliteration, sometimes symmetry of appearance, sometimes antithesis. Of such nature are expressions like "femmes fugaces," (fugaceous females), "le très coquet caméléon de l'entendement," (the very flirtatious chameleon of understanding), "le désert vertical," (the vertical desert), "l'aigle sexuel," (the sexual eagle), "l'adorable déshabillé de l'eau," (the adorable deshabille of the water), "les arêtes des buissons et des navires," (the fishbones of the bushes and the boats), images taken at random from the poetry of Eluard and Breton, the effectiveness of which is entirely dependent on the rhythmic attuneness, generally impossible to carry over into direct translation.

To go one step further, this unexpected linking of words became the foundation of the new metaphor, which, instead of being based on analogy, is derived from divergence and contradiction. A more recent surrealist, Jean Brun, has put it somewhat emphatically in saying in "Le Problème de la sensation et le surréalisme"; "The capital fact of the entire history of the mind lies perhaps in this discovery of surrealism: the word 'comme' is a *verb* which does not signify 'tel que.' " [5] It is a principle to be remembered in reading almost any poem of Breton, Eluard, and most of the other surrealists; it is the trademark of authenticity. It renovates the entire notion of the metaphor, when for instance André Breton can say in *Le Revolver à cheveux blancs*:

The seasons luminous like the interior of an apple from which a slice has been cut out.

[Les saisons lumineuses comme l'intérieur d'une pomme dont on a détaché un quartier.]

A number of years later the technique still persists in René Char's *Le Poème pulvérisé* (1947) when he envisages that the soot of the poker and the crimson of the cloud are but one: "L'encre du tisonnier et la rougeur du nuage ne font qu'un."

The metaphor used to be considered the most effective

means of representing the *image*—which was preconceived in the writer's mind. Now the cart is placed before the horse, and it is the unusual metaphor that creates the even more extraordinary image, which is composed of two or more elements having no logical relationship with each other. One of the first to state the principle clearly was, as we have seen, the so-called cubist poet, Pierre Reverdy, whom the surrealists revered as their master. Breton quoted him in his first manifesto and praises him again in his 1952 review of surrealist outlook, *Entretiens,* for his "magie verbale." Reminiscing about Reverdy's discussions of the nature of the poetic image, Breton esteems him as an even more important theoretician than Guillaume Apollinaire. In *Le Gant de crin* Reverdy had defined the image as the spontaneous meeting of two very distant realities whose relationship is grasped solely by the mind. Reverdy, moreover, observed that the more remote the relationship was between the two realities, the stronger became the resulting image. On the other hand, the power or even the life of the image was threatened if it were to be totally acceptable to the senses. Following this line of thinking, Breton finds that comparison is therefore a poor axis for the image, and that a radical modification is necessary in the very structure of the analogy. The surrealist image has to be a far-fetched chance encounter of two realities whose effect is likened to the light produced by the contact of two electrical conductors. In the ordinary image, the terms of which are chosen on the basis of similarity, the difference in potential between them is negligible and no spark results. The value of the surrealist image, therefore, consists not in an equivalence but in the subtraction of one set of associations from the other. The greater the disparity, the more powerful the light, just as in electricity the greater the difference in potential of the two live wires the greater the voltage. The resulting spark of imagery is first dazzling to the mind, which subsequently accepts and appreciates its reality. Thus by their inadvertent function the metaphors and resulting images increase the poet's scope of understanding of himself, and of the succinct relationships in the world about him. Says René Crevel: "The writer makes his metaphor, but his metaphor unveils, throws light on its author."

Images constructed according to this notion would contain a dose of absurdity and that element of surprise, which, in the opinion of Guillaume Apollinaire, was to be one of the fundamental resources of the modern mind. This type of poetic imagery rises on the same foundation as the "fortuitous meeting," in the words of Max Ernst, of two objects in a surrealist painting as we shall note in detail in the following chapter. The effect that Dali created by placing a telephone and an omelette on the same range of vision in his painting, "Sublime moment," is a result of the same technique as the juxtaposition in a verbal image such as "un couvert d'argent sur une toile d'araignée" (a silver plate on a cobweb) in Breton's poem "Sur la Route qui monte et descend," or the opening lines of *Fata Morgana* (1940):

This morning the daughter of the mountain is holding on her
  knees an accordion of white bats

[Ce matin la fille de la montagne tient sur ses genoux un accordéon de chauves-souris blanches]

In his poem, "L'Union libre," Breton employs what would on the surface appear to be the hackneyed procedure of describing the beauty of the beloved through a series of analogies. Yet the associations of the physical characteristics of the woman are with such unexpected objects as footprints of mice, the brim of a swallow's nest, the slate roof of a hothouse, mist on window panes, cut hay, quicksilver, wet chalk, gladiola, to mention but a few, that the reader is left without the slightest photographic image of the woman but with the spark suggesting her overwhelming power upon the poet.

Breton gave classifications for the surrealist image, for which examples can readily be found in his works and in those of other surrealists.

1. *Contradictions.* For instance in one of his earlier surrealist texts Breton plays on the linguistic contradiction caused by the simultaneous use of the past, present and future tenses to create the impossible phenomenon of the movement of nonexistent curtains on the windows of future houses:

Les rideaux qui n'ont jamais été levés
Flottent aux fenêtres des maisons qu'on construira

In the much later poem, "Tiki" from the group called *Xénophiles,* the same sense of contradiction is conveyed by the combination of two adjectives incompatible in their original concrete meanings though having a junction in their extended connotation:

I love you on the surface of seas
Red like the egg when it is green

[Je t'aime à la face des mers
Rouge comme l'oeuf quand il est vert]

2. *One of the terms of the image is hidden.* This can be noticed in a section of Eluard's "La Rose publique," consisting of a series of incomplete images:

All along the walls furnished with decrepit orchestras
Darting their leaden ears toward the light
On guard for a caress mingled with the thunderbolt

[Le long des murailles meublées d'orchestres décrepits
Dardant leurs oreilles de plomb vers le jour
A l'affût d'une caresse corps avec la foudre]

3. *The image starts out sensationally, then abruptly closes the angle of its compass.* Witness the following line from Breton's "La Mort rose," in which he juxtaposes his dreams with the sound of the eyelids of water and suddenly finishes the image with an unsatisfactory "dans l'ombre":

Mes rêves seront formels et vains comme le bruit
   de paupières de l'eau dans l'ombre.

Under this heading would come all the unsuccessful images which do not measure up to the expectations aroused by the beginning of the metaphor.

4. *The image possesses the character of a hallucination.* Typical of this is the entire poem, "L'Homme approximatiff," of Tristan Tzara with its agglomeration of animal, vegetable, and mineral words, coming every so often to a head in this strange refrain:

for stony in my garments of schist I have dedicated my awaiting
        to the torment of the oxydized desert
        and to the robust advent of the fire

[car rocailleux dans mes vêtements de schiste j'ai voué mon attente
        au tourment du désert oxydé
        au robuste avénement du feu]

Or Michel Leiris' vision of the sun in his "Marécage du sommeil":

When the sun is but a drop of sweat
a sound of bell
the red pearl falling down a vertical needle

[quand le soleil n'est plus qu'une goutte de sueur
un son de cloche
la perle rouge qui tombe le long d'une aiguille verticale]

5. *The image lends to the abstract the mask of the concrete.* In this category would fall at least half of the surrealist images. They are numerous in Breton's poetry. Take for example simple transfers such as the following: eternity incorporated in a wrist watch, life in a virgin passport, thought becoming a white curve on a dark background, lightness shaking upon our roofs her angel's hair.

Or there are double-deckers such as in *Clair de Terre:*

And in my handbag was my dream this smelling salt
that had only been used by the godmother of God.

[Et dans le sac à main il y avait mon rêve ce flacon de sels
Que seule a respirés la marraine de Dieu.]

or his definition of life in *Fata Morgana:*

Life might be the drop of poison
Of non-sense injected into the song of the lark
        over the poppies.

[La vie serait la goutte de poison
Du non-sens introduite dans le chant de l'alouette
        au-dessus des coquelicots.]

6. *The image implies the negation of some elementary physical property.* Eluard will startle his reader by telling him that the earth is blue like an orange; and in Breton's poetry you might hear the sound of wet street lamps or of a bell made of straw, or find him wishing for the sun to come out at night, or be assured that the tree he has chopped down will forever remain green.

7. Finally there is the broad classification which would include *all images that provoke laughter;* such as in Benjamin Péret's "Au bout du monde":

Stupid like sausages whose sauerkraut has already been
        eaten away.

[Bêtes comme des saucisses dont la choucroute a déjà été
mangée.]

or Breton's "Tournesol":

A farm was prospering in the middle of Paris
And its windows opened upon the Milky Way.

[Une ferme prospérait en plein Paris
Et ses fenêtres donnaient sur la voie lactée.]

The composition of a poem is like an upside down
pyramid, beginning with a word or metaphor, leading
to an image and through conscious or unconscious associations to a series of images. Some of these poems consist
of simple series, one image provoking the next one. René
Char's *Artine* begins in this manner—in the bed prepared
for him there were:

an animal wounded and blood-tinged, the size of a *brioche*,
a lead pipe, a blasting wind, a frozen shell, a fired bullet, two
fingers of a glove, an oil spot, there was no prison door, there
was a taste of bitterness, a glassmaker's diamond, a hair, a day,
a broken chair, a silkworm, a stolen object, a line of overcoats,
a green tamed fly, a coral branch, a shoemaker's nail, a wheel
of a bus.

In other cases the images are integrated although their
connections are not logical. Breton's "Au Regard des di-
vinités" is an image-poem that completes a full circle of
interwoven, mystifying metaphors.

"A little before midnight by the waterfront
"If you see a woman all disheveled following your steps
        pay no heed
"It is the azure. You need have no fear of the azure.
"There will be a tall fair vase in a tree
"The steeple of the village with colors mixed
"Will be your rallying point. Take your time
"And remember. The brown geyser that darts into the skies its
                spray of fern
"Salutes you."
                The letter sealed at three corners with a fish
Passed now into the suburban light,
Like a defier's sign
                The while
The beauty, the victim, locally called
The little pyramid of mignonette
Unstitched for herself a cloud like
A sachet of pity
                Later the white armor
Used for household tasks and other things
The unhatched child, the one that was to be
But silence
                A fire has already kindled
In her heart a wild novel of cloaks
And daggers
                On the dock, at the same hour,
Just so the dew balanced its pussy head
The night,—and the illusions would get lost.

Here come the White Fathers from the vespers' mass
The great key hanging over their heads
Here come the grey heralds; and last her letter
Or her lip: my heart is a cuckoo for God

But while she speaks, only the wall is left
Beating in a tomb like a festered veil
Eternity is looking for a wrist watch
A little before midnight by the waterfront.

["Un peu avant minuit près du débarcadère.
"Si une femme échevelée te suit n'y prend pas garde.
"C'est l'azur. Tu n'as rien à craindre de l'azur.
"Il y aura un grand vase blond dans un arbre.
"Le clocher du village des couleurs fondues
"Te servira de point de repère. Prends ton temps,
"Souviens-toi. Le geyser brun qui lance au ciel les pousses de
                              fougère
"Te salue."
            La lettre cachetée aux trois coins d'un poisson
Passait maintenant dans la lumière des faubourgs
Comme une enseigne de dompteur.
                              Au demeurant
La belle, la victime, celle qu'on appelait
Dans le quartier la petite pyramide de réséda
Décousait pour elle seule un nuage pareil
A un sachet de pitié.
                  Plus tard l'armure blanche
Qui vaquait aux soins domestiques et autres
En prenant plus fort à son aise que jamais,
L'enfant à la coquille, celui qui devait être . . .
Mais silence.
                    Un brasier déjà donnait prise
En son sein à un ravissant roman de cape
Et d'épée.
            Sur le pont, à la même heure,
Ainsi la rosée à tête de chatte se berçait.
La nuit,—et les illusions seraient perdues.

Voici les Pères blancs qui reviennent de vêpres
Avec l'immense clé pendue au-dessus d'eux.
Voici les hérauts gris; enfin voici sa lettre
Ou sa lèvre: mon coeur est un coucou pour Dieu.

Mais le temps qu'elle parle, il ne reste qu'un mur
Battant dans un tombeau comme une voile bise.
L'éternité recherche une montre-bracelet
Un peu avant minuit près du débarcadère.]

The poet finds himself in a magnetic field wherein by the
attraction of one image to another the objects of reality
are deviated from their traditional roles. The result is
an incongruous unit which transmits a marvelous vision
of the world, a panorama whose landscapes are picked not
from within the range of the human eye, but from the
combinations with which language can feed the imagination. A good example of this type of poem is Paul Eluard's
"Nous Sommes:"

You see the fire of dusk alighting from its shell
And you see the forest plunged deep in its dew
You see the naked plain on the flank of the trailing sky
The snow high as the sea
And the sea straining toward the azure.

Stones, perfect polish, soft woods, veiled reliefs
You see the cities in tints of melancholy gilt
And sidewalks with excuses overflowing
A spot where loneliness has built its monument
Smilingly, and love its sole abode.

You see the animals
Cunning counterparts to each other sacrificed

Immaculate brethren with shadows intertwined
In a desert of blood.

You see a handsome child playing, laughing
Much smaller he appears
Than the tiny bird at the tip of the twigs

You see a landscape tasting of oil and water
Whence rock is barred, where earth abandons
Its green to summer's blanket of fruitfulness

Women stepping down from their ancient mirror
Bring you their youth and their faith in yours
And one her light the veil which draws you
Makes you see secretly the earth without you

It is with us that all will come to life.

Fauve, my real banners of gold
Plains, my good adventures
Useful pasture throbbing cities
Men will come to lead you.

Men out of the sweat and blows and tears
But who will gather one by one their dreams

I see men, true, feeling, good, useful
Throw off a weight slighter than death
And sleep from joy at the sound of the sun.

[Tu vois le feu du soir qui sort de sa coquille
Et tu vois la forêt enfouie dans la fraîcheur

Tu vois la plaine nue aux flancs du ciel traînard

La neige haute comme la mer
Et la mer haute dans l'azur

Pierres parfaites et bois doux secours voilés
Tu vois des villes teintes de mélancolie
Dorée des trottoirs pleins d'excuses
Une place où la solitude a sa statue
Souriante et l'amour une seule maison

Tu vois les animaux
Sosies malins sacrifiés l'un à l'autre
Frères immaculés aux ombres confondues
Dans un désert de sang

Tu vois un bel enfant quand il joue quand il rit
Il est bien plus petit
Que le petit oiseau du bout des branches

Tu vois un paysage aux saveurs d'huile et d'eau
D'où la roche est exclue où la terre abandonne
Sa verdure à l'été qui la couvre de fruits

Des femmes descendant de leur miroir ancien
T'apportent leur jeunesse et leur foi en la tienne
Et l'une sa clarté la voile qui t'entraîne
Te fait secrètement voir le monde sans toi

C'est avec nous que tout vivra

Bêtes mes vrais étendards d'or
Plaines mes bonnes aventures
Verdure utile villes sensibles
A votre tête viendront des hommes

Des hommes de dessous les sueurs les coups les larmes
Mais qui vont cueillir tous leurs songes

Je vois des hommes vrais sensibles bons utiles
Rejeter un fardeau plus mince que la mort
Et dormir de joie au bruit du soleil.]

By cultivating that very sense of deformity and disproportion which Edgar Allan Poe long before the surrealists had attributed to the poet, they seem to have gone into direct competition with the scientist; for the kind of linguistic reality they grant to the infinite could be likened to the mathematical reality given to the infinite by the number $\frac{1}{0}$ or the concrete symbol of the imaginary in the numerical term of the square root of minus one.

What kind of syntax or sentence structure holds together these images? Here we come to a misconception that often arises concerning the ambiguity of the surrealistic style: the contention that surrealists disdain grammar. The early Dada writings and some of the extreme tongue-in-cheek statements of the surrealists have done much to give this impression. But as Aragon admits, surrealism is not a refuge against style.[8] On the contrary, in the best of their works the surrealists' grammar is impeccable. The most incomprehensible sentence could be parsed, for it is not the structure that is ambiguous but, as we have seen, the mating of words and the incongruous image that results. The surrealists, freed of the exigencies of rhyme, do not have to resort even to the tedious inversions so frequent in classical and romantic verse.

There are two basic structures in the surrealist poem: sentences which follow the conventional order of subject, verb and object, as in most of the poem of Eluard quoted above; or a series of noun or adjective clauses which do not pretend to be parts of complete sentences but succeed each other as if they were enumerations of plain nouns and adjectives. Sometimes the two types of composition are joined into one long sentence or stanza. For example in "L'Homme approximatif," one hundred and twenty-three breath groups form one complete sentence, and nineteen images appear before the principal verb.

The use of verbs is particularly interesting. As Robert Desnos expressed it very appropriately, the tense most often used is the Present.[9] Moreover, there can be noted a preponderance of the simplest verbs: *avoir, être, voir, aimer,* the impersonal *il y a,* which in their imprecision permit the loosest form of bonds between nouns, leaving it to the noun to establish the vision. Another significant use of the verb is the frequent occurrence of the infinitive —noncommittal, democratic, since it favors no particular subject.

The freedom of the imagery is further enhanced by the suppression of words of transition: no *ainsi, donc,*[10] or and the like, since the continuity is outside of the jurisdiction of grammar and lies in the sensory associations of the reader. Indeed by the flexibility of the form the autonomy of the reader, in interpreting the poem, is increased.

In the place of connective words there occurs a great deal of juxtaposition and apposition, producing those stupefying parallels of concurrent realities of which we become aware in this type of writing.

In sum, what essentially separates the surrealist way of writing from the poetry of the preceding generations is *not* its break and emancipation from metrical form; nor does the difference lie in any disregard for grammatical structure. It is, rather, in the use of words: an enrichment of the active vocabulary of poetry, a release from verbal inhibitions, a selection of word association beyond the barriers set up by logic, a new metaphor built upon these incongruous word groupings, and the images resulting from the association of one metaphor with another—which one might call the square of the metaphor. Finally, these images are cast into grammatically accurate sentences connected primarily on the basis of sensual synchronization.

What the surrealists have done is not to sacrifice clarity but to decide that this asset of prose was a liability in poetry. For French had assumed too long with M. Jourdain that what is not prose is verse. Poetry was discovered to be a different type of intellectual activity, consisting of what one might call mental deviation and linguistic alchemy.

It was a terrible test to which language was subjected, a veritable "trial of language" as Aragon had called it. That language which foreign critics have often condemned as unpoetic, as too specific, too rigid to express the ineffable dream vagueness necessary to true poetry, was now being destined to a plane of mystery and irrationalism beyond anything attempted in any of the so-called poetic languages. Recognizing this renaissance of poetry and the linguistic experimentation related to it, Apollinaire had made this challenging statement as early as 1918: "As far as can be seen there are hardly any poets today except of the French language." [11]

It is too early yet to estimate the extent of the transformation surrealism will bring about in the French language, just as the effects of Du Bellay's sixteenth century *Défense et Illustration de la langue française* were not crystallized until the seventeenth century. The surrealists have written too much, confused liberty with license at times, and probably made five unsatisfactory images for every successful one. There has been much trial and error, and unfortunately the surrealists consider every word that falls from their pen so sacred that they have freely published their errors. But the fact remains that their vociferous rejection of standard styles has affected non-surrealists as well as surrealists and is beginning to have an effect on the poetic language of other countries as well. The surrealists consider their experimental work only the beginning of a tremendous upheaval which will test man's ability to integrate his perceptions over and above the miscellany of nature and thereby make of the poetic image not a representation but an invention of the human mind.

It is evident that in coming into contact with this type of poetry words such as *understanding, explanation, expression* are inappropriate. *Knowledge, empathy, dis-*

turbance are the type of terms that best convey the surrealist poet's aspirations.

The crucial difference between previous linguistic revolutions and the surrealist one is that this time the transformation of the word is not an end in itself nor even a means to the more effective communication of what *is,* but what is succinct without the word. Rather, we witness one of the most exciting uses that language has ever been put to: language creates, it makes concrete the ineffable dream, it establishes the promised land, it enables man to discover the absolute that heretofore he had associated with acts of evasion or had to dismiss from earthly experience and relegate to religious conjectures alone. For the surrealist poet, and as we shall note for the surrealist artist as well, the absolute and the infinite are within range of his pen or pencil, dependent on his power over words (or lines), on his ability to shuffle them, seizing their chance meetings, and on the variety of combinations he can produce with them. His mysticism constantly draws on this reservoir of language, and it proves to his wonder that language is such a rich vein that it cannot be exhausted. Through the word, the impossible is made possible, nature can be endowed with metaphysical properties, sensuality takes on new proportions: visions dispersed on the face of the earth, going a-begging, undiscerned in their individual solitudes, are drawn to the new linguistic magnet and brought together into a new synthesis of imagery which in turn creates a new synthesis of existence.

A fundamental and common subject of poetry such as love can be entirely altered and identified not with universal, emotional experience, but with an unusual disturbance of physical surroundings as in Breton's "L'Air de l'eau":

Your flesh sprinkled by the flight of a thousand birds of
      paradise
Is a high flame lying in the snow

[Ta chair arrosée de l'envol de mille oiseaux de paradis
Est une haute flamme couchée dans la neige]

or it can be connected with cosmic awareness:

They say that yonder the beaches are black
With lava lapped up by the sea
And they roll out at the foot of a great snow smoked peak
Under a second sun of wild canaries
What is this far-off land
Which seems to draw its light from your life
It trembles so real at the point of your lids
Kind to your complexion as an immaterial cloth
Just out of the half-open trunk of the ages
Behind you
The ground of a lost paradise
Casting its last dim fires between your limbs
Ice of darkness mirror of love
And lower toward your arms opening
Bringing proof with the spring
To come
Of the nonexistence of evil
The full blossomed apple tree of the sea

[On me dit que là-bas les plages sont noires
De la lave allée à la mer
Et se déroulent au pied d'un immense pic fumant de neige
Sous un soleil de serins sauvages
Quel est donc ce pays lointain
Qui semble tirer toute sa lumière de ta vie
Il tremble bien réel à la pointe de tes cils
Doux à ta carnation comme un linge immatériel
Frais sorti de la malle entr'ouverte des âges
Derrière toi
Lançant ses derniers feux sombres entre tes jambes
Le sol du paradis perdu
Glace de ténèbres miroir d'amour
Et plus bas vers tes bras qui s'ouvrent
A la preuve par le printemps
D'après
De l'inexistence du mal
Tout le pommier en fleur de la mer] [12]

The expression of the eternity of love, essayed by all the eloquence of centuries of poets, seals in Breton's language its indubitable permanence by the simplest and the most effective contradiction of words:

I have found the secret
Of loving you
Always for the first time

[J'ai trouvé le secret
De t'aimer
Toujours pour la première fois] [13]

Saint-Pol-Roux had felt that henceforth art had to consist of invention, but he had not had sufficient resources to accomplish the act of creation. The surrealists found in a linguistic revolution the tool of their earth-bound *mystique*. Whereas it is generally assumed that imagination acquires its resources in remembered realities, the imagination of the surrealists is the power of utilizing words to produce unremembered, previously nonexistent realities—but realities just the same, in the full, concrete, dimensional sense of the word. The abstract words are banished and with them the generalizations of experience. The concrete words kindle in their associations a reality of intensified existence which makes escapism no longer necessary. The *mystique* of language disclosed by the surrealists has as far as the French language is concerned begun the alchemy and bewitchment dreamed of by Baudelaire and Rimbaud, paralleled as yet in no other language, but equalled and sometimes even surpassed in the *mystique* of the line cultivated simultaneously by the artists who participated in the same spiritual crisis and the aesthetic revolution which it released.

N O T E S

1. Aragon, *Traité du style,* Gallimard, Paris, 1928, p. 48.

2. Breton, *Manifestes du surréalisme,* Editions du Sagittaire, 1946, p. 60-1.

3. Michel Leiris, "Glossaire," *Révolution Surréaliste,* III, pp. 6-7.

4. Arpad Mezei, *Le Surréalisme en 1947* (Edition Pierre à Feu), 1947, p. 59.

5. Jean Brun, "Le Problème de la sensation et le surréalisme," *Ibid.,* p. 90.

6. Breton, *Les Manifestes du surréalisme,* Sagittaire, 1946, p. 63.

7. Breton, "Textes surréalistes," *Révolution Surréaliste,* VI, p. 6.

8. Aragon, *Traité du style,* p. 189.

9. Robert Desnos, "Confession d'un enfant du siècle," R.S., VI, p. 18.

10. Breton tells us in "Signe ascendant" that he detests the word "donc," p. 112 in *La Clé des champs.*

11. Apollinaire, "L'Esprit nouveau et les poètes," *Mercure de France,* Dec. 1, 1918, p. 394.

12. Breton, *Poèmes,* Gallimard, Paris, 1948, p. 148.

13. *Ibid.,* p. 150.

the surrealist object

—the eyes must reflect what is not—*André Breton*

The upheaval of the word was to have its counterpart in the crisis of the object. Early in the century Apollinaire had discerned that the essential intention of the cubists was an almost metaphysical leap in space lifting the object from nature's frame and reorienting it in the infinite. In *Les Peintres cubistes* Apollinaire was not afraid of attributing the label "religious" to the "inhuman" effort of the artist to bridge the gap between imitation and creation. Although like Saint-Pol-Roux, Apollinaire was becoming aware that henceforth all artists must join in a common aspiration to attain a superhuman degree of imagination, the artist rather than the poet took the first step in turning the wish into reality. The concepts of Lautréamont and Rimbaud were to be illustrated in art before they reached maturation in poetry, but it was also the poets who turned out to be the best critics of that art and recorded the consciousness of creation behind the work of art.

In his poems inspired by Picasso's art Paul Eluard gave the artist his most powerful tribute when he pictured him endowed in God-like fashion with the power not to *reveal* visions but to *provoke* them, giving sight a new potential: making the act of seeing more important than the object to be seen.

In his remarkable book of art criticism, *Le Surréalisme et la peinture,* André Breton is so overwhelmed with the debt owed to Picasso, that he includes him in the surrealist fold and would like to have the label of cubist removed from him.

But what Breton would do in a spasm of enthusiasm must be somewhat modified in the cooler atmosphere produced by the passage of time. There is the same type of gap between the surrealists and the cubists in art as between the dadaists and the surrealists in poetry. Picasso and Braque, as well as the early Chirico, began primarily as destroyers rather than creators. Picasso, sensing the need to deviate from the accepted form of the object, distorted it, brought to it different perspectives simultaneously, or dissected it, made it unrecognizable. Chirico altered the climate of both living and inanimate forms, denuded the frame, created a vacuum in which sparse objects pause as if in finality, shedding their known robes and acquiring new ones that must be guessed. The simplest figures became the most mystifying because of the unrestrictive character of simplicity.

But Chirico stopped at the limit of space and later deviated, to the disappointment of the surrealists, into more acceptable channels, while Picasso continued to keep his emphasis on deformation.

It is the later generation with its two-fold artistic and poetic inspiration that was to produce the crisis of the model and then proceed to a radical mutation of the object. In its work it was immeasurably aided by André Breton and his coterie of writers whose experiments with the word had a tremendous effect on the new consideration of the object.

Never had a non-artist, not even Baudelaire, been so closely linked with art-creation as Breton. In his opinion these artists, gathered from various parts of Europe, constituting an even more international group than the surrealist writers, were bringing about a spiritual revolution on a level with the mathematical upheaval caused by the advent of non-Euclidian mathematics. They were to be inventors, as Saint-Pol-Roux had sensed, marking a very evolved step in the development of the human mind: the possession of the ability to enlarge and control its sense perceptions.

In his penetrating articles on "Surrealism and Painting,"

and particularly in "Genesis and Artistic Perspective of surrealism," Breton states that the emancipation of the object is the result of the artist's release from the obsession of usage. The important thing for the artist is not to see or hear but to *recognize*. Finding support in Rimbaud's comments about the poetic vision, Breton believes that instead of seeking the actual, current appearances of things, one must look for the latent significance. This does not imply that one must search for rare objects; often the simplest ones are the most enigmatic, the most charged with possible contacts with our mental activity, so that actually the things that surround us are not really objects but become the subjects of our spiritual environment. But their subjective quality does not deprive them of their concrete dimensions. Instead of purifying them into a state of abstraction, the artist quite to the contrary, attempts to heighten their substantial reality.

Just as the surrealists conducted experimental activities with the high voltage of words, so they combined forces with artists such as Giacometti, Dali, and Max Ernst to acquire an unexpected knowledge of objects, by discovering the representative range and power of certain objects such as a silver bowl, a piece of velvet, a painting of Chirico. The important thing was not the choice of object as much as the circumstances of its viewing and its location or position in relation to other things or beings. They called their experiment: "Research on irrational knowledge of the object." Its principal purpose was to destroy the conventional value of the object and to replace it by a representative value, just as the usual connotation of the word, as we saw in the previous chapter was replaced by another one, perhaps closer to the primitive meaning. Through adroit questions and spontaneous reactions it was revealed to what extent the object could be related to the psychic life of the viewer. The intensity of the psychic stimulus is judged by the vividness and richness of associations which it arouses.

The laboratory experiment, moved to the plane of artistic production, sets new standards of values for the artist's work. Instead of the age-old adherence to a faithful representation of familiar objects and landscapes, the surrealist painter seeks a new objective. His success is to be judged by the degree of fusion the work permits between the ability to perceive, and the inner hallucination that is set in motion and given a concrete representation. It can be seen how closely pictorial and verbal creativeness are thus linked.

This was not an attempt to transcend the physical world but to transmute it, not to rise above but to change at will the climate by rejecting the entities which do not coordinate with the artist's inner world and by concentrating on those that did. When, therefore, the common denominator of perception is erased and replaced by a purely subjective grasp, the objects bear the same estrangement from accepted standards of perspective as the actual perception of one individual differs from another's. The world, and therefore the work, of each artist bears his exclusive stamp and can resemble no other and by the same token can readily be distinguished from all the rest.

The mind no longer accepts the data of the sensations

but controls them by directing the eye and the touch. The perception thereby attained is not something abstract but very material. Breton points out that surrealist art is very far removed from the abstract or from so-called "pure" art, which on the contrary dematerializes the object into an idea. It also becomes quite evident that the artist has wandered far from symbolism and impressionism. The generalization of role that the symbol bestows on the concrete is the exact reverse of the character of the surrealist art object which is a study in the particular delivering the object from its general role or giving it a specialized new one. This attitude is close to the situation noted in Reverdy's poetry in which the world was seen full of unfamiliar objects, or familiar ones that expressed the unknown, rather than as a forest of familiar symbols. Of such deviated, changed objects the daily marvels of the earth are composed for the artist. In their power of stimulation they can surpass the mystical dreams of the past. This is the same "merveilleux quotidien" that illuminated the Paris of Aragon in *Le Paysan de Paris*. The poet had come to the realization that he could be a materialist without being a determinist: accept the objective reality of matter but not allow it to be interpreted merely by his rational faculties. When material reality could be grasped by the united efforts of reason and imagination, then the poet could become a visionary of the miracles in the field of reality which far surpassed those of legend or those of pure fantasy. But this exercise of the mental qualities implied that the word imagination was to be given a new connotation—it was not to be any longer subservient to memory but was to feed on a deep-set psychic intuition. This poetic position was appropriated by the artists as well when they realized that the power of objects could be enhanced in the same manner as the power of words.

The artist's mind and eye, as the poet's, were subjected to rigorous training. Henceforth, the artist's hands were to create the objects projected from his mind, after its process of selection and alchemy: "what is seen in him," just as the poet's pen transcribed, at times insensibly, the dictates of his metaphoric vision. Art, even as poetry, was to become not an escape from the narrowness of lived reality, but the overflow of intensified life experience. Characterizing vision as frustrated or impaired Paul Nougé explained in his article on "Les Images défendues" (The Forbidden Images) which appeared in the fifth issue of *Le Surréalisme au Service de la Révolution,* that the artist can enrich his existence by recognizing and learning to control the freedom of the eye: "The eye that still sees what no longer is, the star; on the screen the vanished image; which does not see what passes too rapidly, the bullet, this smile; which does not see what is too slow, the grass that grows, old age; who recognizes a woman and it's another one, a cat and it is a shoe, his love and it is emptiness—the freedom of the eye should have warned us long ago."

Observing in retrospect the writings of this massive alliance of artists and poets of that most creative period between the two world wars, one becomes aware that the greatest quality of surrealist work was the evidence it gave of the remarkable level and intensified use of all known mental faculties and the exploration of latent ones. The artist, whether through the word or through the line, who could establish the most intimate relationship between exterior reality and his inner world was deemed the most successful creator of the aesthetic absolute, the most to be envied, the most to be extolled. The degree of closeness was obviously dependent on the flexibility and adaptability of the imaginative faculty. Dali defined the creative works thus conceived as "meteors of imagination."

But beyond that, the artist must also have the ability to arouse in the spectator the curiosity to grasp his image. In the same article quoted above, Paul Nougé said: "it is not enough to create an object, it is not enough for it to be. We must show that it can, by some artifice, arouse in the spectator, the desire, the need to see." When the painting no longer acts as a sedative but as a stimulus, arrests the mind in its restless dissatisfied wanderings, and fixes its attention in a position of significant immobility, similar perhaps to the stillness of a religious ecstasy, and concentrates it so intensely that the viewer ceases to see at random in order to recognize his own power of creative transfiguration of the universe, then indeed the work of art has achieved its moment of miracle. Not escape, not sublimized emotion, are then the objectives of the work of art, but the creation of this kind of communication which Breton has called "convulsive" beauty and which Paul Nougé identified with the sense of the marvelous: "The marvel is embodied. An unforeseen evidence joins with bonds of flesh and blood his (the spectator's) disconnected limbs. In this fashion does the painting sometimes exist." If this miraculous empathy can occur at all it is because all men at some time or another are subject to the profound need of deviating from the circuit of the orderly connection between things, and the greatest revelation that can come to them is to discover that they are not hermetically sealed within it.

It may be an anomaly that at the very moment when science was challenging the established gamut of the human imagination by the dazzling effect of its rationalizations, the poet and the artist refused to be left on the defensive, and instead, joined forces to reassert faith, if not in the products of imagination, certainly in its power. We have noted the method of exercise of the poetic imagination and its literary manifestation; the artistic feats displayed the same pitch of philosophic concern and mental orientation.

The most obvious demonstration of the irrational understanding of objects is their distortion in the work of art. Cubists and early surrealists give the most frequent evidence of this occurrence. Picasso's "Guitar, Fish and Bottles," dating from his early period, later ones such as "Bird in Branch," or "Vase of Flowers," are striking illustrations of this principle; so are Dali's melting watches, Max Ernst's furnace-like mass called "The Elephant of Célèbes."

The distortion does not stop with things or animals. It takes on a more dramatic significance with the repre-

sentation of humans. In Picasso the tendency became his
pictorial signature and ran a wide range of variations
from simple facial distortions and double perspectives of
full face and profile, to complete destruction of the human form, a veritable dehumanization, which was to become one of the points of departure of the surrealists.
Picasso's busts of women where just the faces are disturbed are followed or supplemented by others in which
the body is not constructed but deciphered, reduced to its
functions, with particular violence done to the breasts;
the softness that circular line suggests is suddenly transformed into hardness by the abrupt manner in which
the circle is placed on the cold frame, or elongated and
adjusted with nails as in "Woman in Chemise."

Man's reduction to the level of things was demonstrated in the most total way, of course, in the works of
Marcel Duchamp: his nudes, his virgins, his newly-weds,
all indicating perhaps his basic inclination to fuse the
process of physical creativeness with the power of artistic
creation. Miró's curved lines echo Duchamp's straight
ones, jumbled representations such as "Portrait of Madame
Mills in 1750," or "Head of a Woman."

The dehumanization is complicated in Max Ernst's
paintings by a merging of human and animal characteristics as in "Portrait voilé." This process is also inherent
in the creation of new living beings attempted by many
of the artists of this cubist-early surrealist epoch: the
ghost concepts of the twentieth century, such as the early
model of the "Vaticinateur" of Chirico, or the later un-
earthly model of Dali, called "Le Grand Mastubateur."

Paul Eluard, commenting on this technique in his book, *Picasso*, calls this distortion of the natural human line an effort to integrate the universe:

"Language is a social fact. But may we not hope that one day design, like language, like writing, will become so; and with these will pass from social to the universal plane? All men will communicate through the vision of things; and that vision of things will serve them to express the point that is common to them: to them, to things, to them as things, to things as them. On that day, a true clairvoyance will have integrated the universe to man —that is to say, man to the universe." [1]

A final aspect of dehumanization is the total disappearance of man from his portrait. He finds himself represented simply by the objects which characterize him. Here again the pioneers are Chirico and Picasso, in works such as "The Evil Genius of a King," and "Glass, Pipe and Matches," or in the more subtle and evolved forms that representation takes in Dali's "Invisible Man," where his mind's images are projected into concrete line and form, and in Joan Miró's "Le Chasseur," where the notions of aim and target are the crystallization of the function represented.

Although this attack on the human form, a pronounced characteristic of the surrealist image, is a radical departure from the technique of imitation in art, it is only an initial step in the lifting of the silvering from the artist's mirror. The next steps are more intricate, more germane to surrealism, and demonstrate more clearly the schism between cubism and surrealism.

Distortion is at most a narrow field of composition. Although the outer image represents the inner eye, in art as in poetry the mere representation of images is not a rich expression of creativeness and may eventually lead to attrition. It suggests an inbred, circumscribed world. If, as so much evidence suggests, the modern artist's and poet's basic motivation is an inclination toward mysticism, the relationships in the outer world must not be limited to their connections with the inner self, but on the contrary have to be envisaged in a broader network of mutual associations on the objective plane of reality. The object is the unit, as the word was seen to be a unit in the previous chapter, but the integrated vision rises no more out of the object than it did out of the word. Rather, it comes out of the metaphor, which translated into art, means the possibilities of association between objects.

In its simplest form this means that single objects can be seen to contain elements of dual association or function. For example Victor Brauner's "Woman as a Cat" incorporates catlikeness into the eye, the hand, and produces as it were a double flower sprouting from the breast. One of the most provoking of this type of dual image is Dali's "Apparition of face and fruit-dish on a beach" where the outer limit of the eye structure is the bottom of the bowl, and the table on which the bowl rests assumes the fluctuations of the face it latently contains.

But the next level of development is much more fertile. As we have seen, the verbal surrealism of poetry rests on the linking of images that destroy the conjunction "as" and seek their bases of association in haphazard and chance meetings of ideas and visions, made possible by the free volleying of thought rather than by reason. Similarly, in pictorial art we find the unexpected juxtaposition of objects whereby the inner eye creates its own composite and concrete vision of the objective world. It is noteworthy that the poets were not alone in having recourse to the poetic pronouncements of a previous generation. Where the poets leaned heavily on Saint-Pol-Roux and Reverdy, the artists particularly clung to—and made famous—a statement of Lautréamont as the crux of their objective in art:

"Beautiful like the fortuitous meeting, on a dissection table, of a sewing machine and an umbrella."

Out of it Max Ernst developed his famous formula of "the fortuitous meeting of distant realities" going a step further in declaring that all such associations were to have a purely temporary status and might surrender at any moment to new combinations. The process is described in detail by André Breton in his discussion of the art of Max Ernst in his *Le Surréalisme et la peinture:* "to assemble these dissimilar objects according to an order which was different from theirs and . . . to avoid as much as possible all preconceived plan." [2]

These chance encounters were stimulated by automatic drawing and "collage." The first result was the weird estrangement of the object, produced by its separation from the objects that have generally adhered to it, sheltered or nurtured it. This might be called the coming of age of the object, weaned from its source, left to seek out relations other than the familiar ones. The sense of detachment created by the object's new position in outer reality corresponded to the inner isolation that the artist and poet have felt in the present century despite their coteries and fraternal, collective aspirations. But the break with inner and outer links did not leave them long in a sterile vacuum. The new associations in pictorial representation were to be as highly charged in voltage as the verbal ones.

Since this is the basic technique of surrealist art the examples are too numerous to cite. It forms the core of Dali's surprises, "absurdities," challenges, ludicrous ones such as "A Chemist lifting with extreme precaution the cuticle of a grand piano," or subtle, provocative ones like "Aerodynamic Chair" in which a seat is hoisted on top of an autumnal tree against whose trunk is placed a nude woman and a dresser with a backdrop of water and mountain suggesting the desolation of volcanic aridity.

The juxtaposition in Marc Chagall's "Time has no shores" is the succinct marriage of such distant realities as a fish, a violin, a hand and a swinging pendulum cracking down into a countryside, and in its shadows, a couple making love undisturbed. In the cosmic fresco-like paintings of Max Ernst the juxtaposition sometimes reaches cataclysmic proportions whereby the free intermingling of objects eventually causes a breakdown of the barriers between the vegetable, mineral and animal reigns, as for example in "Nature at Dawn."

Once the barriers are down and a new promiscuity has been established between exterior entities heretofore relegated to separate planes, the next step is the overflow of the nonform abstract image into a concrete objective existence, not the abstraction in art, but just the opposite, the materialization of the abstract, the crystallization of the mental image.

The distortions of form and perspective, and the absurdities of unexpected object associations, can be used as means of conveying mental hallucinations, dream images, simulation of insanity (as in the case of Dali's paranoiac paintings), and most important: the mystic vision divorced from religious symbolism.

Of this character are Man Ray's "Primacy of Matter on Thought," tangibility of form melting into the fluidity of abstraction; the ornate mysticism of Ernst's "L'Oeil du silence" with multiple eyes emanating from stone, and top-heavy gargoyles resting on abysmal waters of silence.

Dali's "Symbol of Anguish," his "Accommodations of Desire," his "Persistence of Memory," translate into concrete reality the silent but tense conflict between measured time and the unaccountable infinite. Perhaps one of the most potent metaphysical images thus composed by Dali, and one of the simplest as far as drawing, is the one called "The Feeling of Becoming," in which man hides all but his head behind a sheet-like curtain held up against the forces of gravity and casting a shadow over distant rocks while it acts itself as a foil to an unexpected shadow of something no doubt present in the unseen foreground.

But despite the originality of such artistic concepts and their execution, the technique so far described and illustrated in surrealist paintings is a semi-compromise with reality. The shape is changed, the forms are mingled freely, the concrete is associated with the abstract, but imagination is still largely conditioned by known experience or entities.

A more total creativeness occurs when an attempt is made at virtual fabrication of new objects and thereafter in their intermingling in an atmosphere all their own, governed by new laws of perspective, and against a new visual horizon. The most evolved forms of surrealist art are concerned with such metaphysical objects and their space-horizon locale in what would seem to be a non-oxygen atmosphere.

The most vivid illustration of this type of surrealist art is René Magritte's "Le Modèle rouge" which starts by being a foot and ends up with the properties of a boot. It is not a double object, suggesting at the same time a woman and a cat or a face and a bowl as in the examples previously cited. This time the object has a fantastic unity as it appears before the viewer: it reposes on pebbles, neither with the pressure of a foot nor that of a boot, but with a weight all its own, suggesting uncanny functions which cannot be associated with any known ones. The container (the boot) and the thing contained (the foot) have achieved an entirely new reality as a new object.

The pursuit of the original object became a collective preoccupation of the surrealists in all fields of artistic expression. Miró populated his paintings with these strange forms, contingent upon each other though completely incompatible with each other in matters of shape, color or size. Giacometti actually constructed new objects, tactile in their suspended position, dimensionally accurate as an engineer's composition, but intended to satisfy a dream-need rather than a rational one. Breton, as always the recorder of surrealist activities called them "phantom objects" and has demonstrated his own such fabrication in surrealist expositions.

As one contemplates the whole range of surrealist expression, the objects and landscapes of Tanguy tower as the most creative manifestations of the entire phantasmal gallery. Tanguy's groupings and enigmatic spaces between objects seem to have been guided to their positions by a sort of divine chance. They suggest spasmodic shocks of atom movements and carry their long shadows before them as if lit up by a sun low in the heavens or as if the sun were below them and not above. Groupings seem to possess separate horizons suspended in a sphere freed of measured time. The colors appear to be those of mingled spectrums of two different suns whose beams might perchance have crossed: ruddy tints of oxidation lacking all character of warmth, and blues not of azure but of mineral.

The mingling of the concrete and the abstract, which we noted in the poetry of surrealism, is brilliantly illustrated both in the titles used by Tanguy such as "Le Temps meublé," or "Le Ruban des excès" and in the paintings themselves where shapes are strikingly three-dimensional and at times seem to pop out of their nonsubstantial frames.

He can suggest hallucinations as the tormented whirlpools of "L'Humeur des temps." Tanguy displays versatile, unexpected juxtapositions, confusing our sense of proportion as in his "Un Grand Tableau qui représente un paysage," or by creating discordances in form through the promiscuity of incompatible shapes. One of his most frequent metaphysical techniques is to confound the laws of gravity, leaving things suspended in the furrows of his skies, or we are faced by the uncanny phenomenon of seeing an object fly down the sky instead of up, in a landscape which he calls—ironically one might say— "Vieil Horizon."

Here we are as close to facing pure creation as has been given to anyone in the realm of the arts. As one gazes at Tanguy's canvases one has the feeling that if man ever achieves his desire to be projected into outer space and on to other planets, what he will find in other worlds and in the distances between them must resemble the objects devised by Yves Tanguy: his flight will be as free of gravity as the positions and attitudes of these objects on Tanguy's canvases. Suspended without accompanying motion as in "Les Amoureux," he will perhaps partake of Tanguy's mystical vision: strata of neither solid nor liquid consistency, the heavy leaning upon the light weight, a semi-light and its self-contained shadows, shapes suggesting dolmens and cactus but with a relationship to the world that is neither that of the plant nor of a stone, for the substance on which they repose is neither earth nor air, containing the colors of silence or of an arctic sunset.

In a telling evolution that can be discerned in Tanguy's work, the objects of his imagination become heavier, more jagged in form, the colors more clashing. Getting larger, closer to the foreground the objects lose more and more the freedom of their space separation. Heavier and lower the objects move in the frame until in his final, immense painting called "Multiplication of the Arcs," completed just before his death, the objects piled upon each other, asphyxiating in their crowded proximity, suggest the final counting of the numbers as he takes stock for the last time of the entities of his universe. As one contemplates these metaphysical landscapes one realizes that Tanguy's unconditional acceptance of matter as the sole but infinite end took him from one anguished level of inanimate objects to another, in their unearthliness denying that quality of the earthly and the human that the surrealist in all forms of art have refused to accept: the notion of the *finite*. Although their critical minds and impetuous personalities had originally found so much to reject in the world, the surrealists were eventually able to adapt their surroundings to their dream by concentrating their rebellion upon one unacceptable concept, the notion of finitude. This rejection is vividly evident in Tanguy's paintings just as it is eloquently expressed in Aragon's words: "the idea of limit is the only inconceivable idea." In the long run, it is also indicative of the basic character of our age.

As one observes the imitators of Ernst, Dali, and lately even of Tanguy, multiply all over the world, one feels their synchronization with the scientist's projection of his instruments and eventually of his person into outer space. One tends to agree with artist-philosopher Ernst that "In yielding quite naturally to the vocation of pushing back appearances and disturbing the relationships of realities, it (the genius of the artist) has contributed with a smile on its lips to the speeding up of the general crisis of conscience which must come to a head in our time." [3]

The apocryphal aspect of the universe in a Tanguy painting is more relevant to our time than the angels of Raphaël, for it conveys in succinct eloquence modern man's current obsession: to extricate himself from the established order of earth-bound measurements and to discover a new relationship between his mortal self and the immortal reality with which he considers himself in daily contact.

Only man is vanity, all else enduring, is the conclusion one might reach as one contemplates these works of art from which little by little man and his relationship with other humans vanishes, giving way to the things that might survive him, perpetuating his imprint, just as the scientist's instruments outreach the vision of his human eyes. In both cases there is produced a vicarious sort of transcendence, which may perhaps lay the foundations of a new metaphysics.

N O T E S

1. Paul Eluard, *Pablo Picasso,* translated by Joseph T. Shipley, Philosophical Library, N.Y., 1947, p. 40.

2. Breton, *Le Surréalisme et la peinture,* Brentano, N.Y., 1945, p. 55.

3. Max Ernst, "Comment on force l'inspiration," *Le Surréalisme au Service de la Révolution,* no. 6, p. 45. (the final sentence of the article).

the bend in the road

◑

the post-*surrealism of*

aragon and eluard

Surrealism has come to have two meanings: it was originally the closely-knit spiritual union of artists and writers who operated under the common trademark, worked out their artistic problems together, wrote for the same periodicals, sometimes even collaborated on works. But as we have seen, in its broader sense it represents a spiritual crisis which stems from the ideological developments of the nineteenth century, and which in our time succeeded in producing a technique of writing and painting to convey a materio-mystical vision of the universe. When just prior to World War II Aragon and Eluard broke up with André Breton they obviously ceased to be "surrealists" in the limited sense of the word; but were they able to shed so lightly and so abruptly the surrealist state of mind which had served as the original motivation for their writing?

Too often the negative influences that helped shape the surrealist movement are mistaken for its positive precepts. In the preface to an anthology of Aragon's poetry (1946) Claude Roy attributed the "fecundity of surrealism" and its appeal to basically different personalities, to an inner contradiction in the character of the movement: a will to change the world versus a wish to give up the world for a nirvana. It is true that the surrealists had two aims, but I do not think that there was any real conflict between them; for the will to change and the will to renounce did not refer to the same type of existence.

The young surrealists of 1920 reacted nihilistically to a certain atmosphere: the smug urbane world whose limited logic they held responsible for war and social chaos. These young men, unlike their elders Claudel, Péguy, and Maurras, found no inspiration in war. When the newly organized surrealists were deriding established traditions and institutions, they were condemning what to them symbolized bigotry and lack of vision. When, at a banquet in honor of Saint-Pol-Roux, a surrealist fanatic cried out "A bas la France!" he was referring to the "France" in the throes of post-war failures.

The surrealists were tired not only of the social status quo but of the literary one as well; they coupled, therefore, their anti-social behavior with artistic anarchism. To them the inefficacy of language had been as responsible for the stagnation of society as the fallibility of thought and action. Literature had been too easy, too wordy. The artistic revolution intimated in the works of Baudelaire and Rimbaud had been side-tracked and muffed by the philosophical abstractions of Academicians and by the rarefied imagery of the symbolists. As Aragon points out in his *Chroniques du Bel Canto* (1947), the fundamental motivation of the new poetry, regardless of names and labels, could have been more broadly summed up as "rimbaldisme." The early surrealist antagonism to language was the antidote to the poetry of the two preceding generations, which on the whole had deviated from the course indicated by Rimbaud.

This double attack aimed at the society and literature of the beginning of the twentieth century had an essentially circumstantial character. Of the positive credo that the surrealists had been developing at the same time, there was only one element manifest in the iconoclastic demonstrations which had gained so much notoriety: the courage to be uncompromising.

If surrealism had just been a means of expressing youthful revolt and rejection, one could be persuaded by Aragon's assertion: "I have never been part of a school," in the preface to his World War II poems, *En Etrange Pays dans mon pays lui-même,* that he was no longer a surrealist. But Aragon's early affiliation had not been merely a social or aesthetic rebellion of youth. He had been deeply involved in the metaphysical anguish of those surrealists who sought to transform this world to satisfy their longing for the absolute. It is not his word but his work which can best attest the extent to which he actually deviated from the surrealist point of view in his later life.

In 1939 Louis Aragon was mobilized; his long record of unpatriotic acts (five years before he had been arrested for publicly insulting the flag) caused him to be kept under the watchful eyes of the authorities; a year later, after having gone through every harrowing experience of the defeat of the French army, he was discharged with three of the highest decorations. Soon there began to appear in various periodicals in the unoccupied zone of France poems he had written during the "phoney" war, and during the early months of his stay in Carcassonne following his demobilization. Later collected under the title of Le Crève-coeur, these poems relate the dreary months of waiting behind the lines, his anxiety in being separated from his wife, the tragic retreat, the soldier-poet's anguish upon hearing of the surrender of Paris on a mild evening in Normandy where the bouquets of retreat were borne to him on the sweet breath of roses in bloom; gardens of France, lilacs of Flanders, stood out in dismal irony in the whirlpool of images that crowded the poet's senses as fear sped the army's flight back. Out of the disaster, poetry surges with an urgent mission which Aragon is not abashed to call "noble"; for poetry seems to him the last foothold on dignity left in his moment of abject humiliation. In his youth he had derided the

photographer's realism; now he was no longer loath to
beat the camera's lens at its own game as he described
the defeat of his country. In the years of the occupation
he continued to write of his love for his country and for
his wife. The late subversive, instead of collaborating with
the enemy, as might have been expected from his peace-
time performance, became a fervent patriot, the morale
builder of the French people, the bard of the United Na-
tions, a backbone of the Resistance.

But when pictures of heroism, devastation, treason, as-
sassination, pillage, murder, human separations invaded
the works of Aragon did they indicate a return to nar-
rative verse, and a recapture of classical eloquence?

Quite the contrary. The surrealist state of mind pre-
vails in the majority of these writings. Once, in philosophical splendor, Aragon had imagined "the concrete
form of disorder"[1] as the outer limit of what the human mind could grasp. Now, confronted with a more
complete disorder than dreamed of in his philosophy, he
set out to capture it poetically as no camera could register
it. In his days of orthodoxy Aragon had defined surrealism as "the unruly and ardent use of the stupefying image"[2] which, he believed, continually revised our entire
universe. Now he created the stupefying image of disaster, together with its numerous associations, which expressed better than words of despair the mournful transformation of his world.

In *Le Crève-coeur, Les Yeux d'Elsa, Cantique à Elsa,
La Diane française* and *Le Musée Grevin* Aragon's picture of the retreat, the surrender, and the occupation is a

pool of concrete images, disjunct or in ironic contradiction to each other: brilliant colors of flowers, interspersed
with deep shadows of death; sweet breath of flowers borne
on a whirlwind of panic; the echo of tanks, the enigmatic
silence of waiting; bouquets of retreat, red as the roses
of Anjou, red as the fires of destruction. His country is a
bark abandoned by its oarsmen; his people's blood is a
wine of poor vintage; the people, the pastures, the dreams
all intermingled, juxtaposed, on a single level of reality.
In the moment of loss he takes stock of his daily surroundings and becomes aware of their eternal significance.
Already keenly conscious of the important role of the
poet, he sees poetry as an elemental need:

> The humming of a song that lightens the tread of heavy feet
> A demi-tasse at dawn
> A friend encountered on the road to the grave.[3]

Among his war poems the surest literary merit belongs
to *En Français dans le texte* and *Brocéliande,* collected
in 1947 under the telling title of *En Etrange Pays dans
mon pays lui-même.* Written in 1942, they employ the
subtlety of double-entendre to trick the censor, and
double meaning suited perfectly the surrealist talent for
avoiding the obvious. Thanks to the censor, Aragon es-
caped in these poems that easy realism to which he occasionally resorted in his earlier war verse. In these series
of poems he raises the incidents to a plane of universality
by using one of the basic techniques of surrealism: the
exploration of the myth which replaces the circumstan-

tial reality of history with the metaphysical reality of the legend:

Since the assayers of gold have closed up their counters
And all greatness has passed us by
I'll take you back Legend and make you my History

The "peasant of Paris," who had had to resort to artificial devices to change the peaceful metropolis into something marvelously different in his earlier days, utilizes in many of these poems all his verbal powers of association to create *in absentia* a new hymn to Paris by means of a series of pictures of the city which the war had forced him to leave. Not tears, not the thoughts, but the avalanche of images tell the story: events are liberated from their tape measures of time, and past and present heroes intermingle, the invisible becomes visible, the vast lines parallel the tiny detail; the exalted is mated with the absurd, the permanent with the transitory: Notre-Dame rising above the Seine like a magnet, boxes of sardines lying desolately on display; the terribly concrete reality of absence in the sound of loosened shutters beating against window panes; objects left absurdly well-arranged in an atmosphere of disorder. Despite the frequent lack of transition or continuity between the metaphors, they pool their resources to create an unforgettable unity of impression.

Brocéliande, the forest of Brittany, where once reigned the magician Merlin of Celtic mythology, gave Aragon his best opportunity for using myth to express the catastrophe of his country. Here, the self-avowed materialist conjured up all the mystical resources of pagan marvels, Christian miracles, and the wonders of man-made machinery to convey the supertemporal image of destruction and regeneration, which the combined evidences of all his senses and the expression of his deepest emotions were not, by themselves, able to relate. Just as he had felt that poetry was not to be retained in an ivory tower but be shared by all, he came to realize that the marvelous which he had sought as the treasured possession of the privileged, was really the legacy of all. He chided those who were "drowning at the port-holes of hope" and invited them "to open up for us their enchanted forests." It was an invitation to dreaming in the midst of unbearable reality:

"Impossible is a word that's banished from the earth." The legend was part of France's national existence. It was, therefore, its truth. In evoking it one would be passing it from one generation to another so that "not one moment may the dreams remain unemployed."

The wondrous hail, the curse of the locust, and modern bombs assume a single reality as they evoke simultaneously the odor of death and of moss in the magical forest. They give destruction a three-edged reality, until finally the stone cries for mercy. The eventual resurrection of the people is either that of Christ, or that of Orpheus; there is no difference for Aragon, to him both hold the veracity of the myth. The regeneration is accompanied by a reawakening of earth and the miracle of multiple harvests. It is a composite symbol of France, possessed on one temporal level of all her past and present legend and reinforced by the salutary vision of her future.

Aragon's basic qualities as man and artist were revealed here: his social consciousness which sought to alter the unwanted reality of the circumstances, and at the same time his artist's clash with the temporal situation; for the poet was defending with a single stroke his two most precious possessions: civic liberty and the liberty to dream as an artist. The dream had been a war casualty too, the dream had been deemed a crime, put in quarantine; to preserve its liberty it had to go underground, for it refused to remain inactive. The visions in *Brocéliande* signal the rescue and presage the victory of the other freedom.

What Eluard wrote during the trying years could also fall into two groups: the directly circumstantial verse representing the basic local color of events and his subtler interpretations of the disaster. In *Vérité et Poésie* and *Au Rendezvous allemand,* the militant tone of anger and indignation sometimes overpowers the surrealist manner. *Le Livre ouvert,* a selection of poems written between 1938 and 1944, includes fewer of the heavily documented pieces. But whether Eluard was describing the defeat of Paris or the less obvious consequences of the disaster, he generally retained his basic surrealist tendency to disregard arbitrary divisions between the concrete and abstract worlds. Even the essentially circumstantial poem "Liberté," whose timeliness and simplicity of language gave it a fame beyond its literary merit, was brought into

the surrealist orbit of perception by the breaking down
of the abstract concept into series of images whose common denominator consists of the subconscious associations they hold with his notion of liberty. Except when
indignation makes him lose his identity as an artist, his
word-images of good and evil, life and death, poverty
and fear, or even the undefinable word "misère" are vivid
metaphors representing distortions of perspective, undulations or splurges of color, a sudden brilliance, a striking
detail.

Ever since the days of his "miroir sans tain" (the mirror without silvering) [4] Eluard had been an expert at ma-
terializing the invisible. Obsessed more than ever by the
presence of death, which he has considered the greatest
challenge to the human imagination, he succeeded in
representing its earthly presence in other than negative
terms. He coordinated the subjective and objective hol-
lows which the dead have created in the material world
when with reluctance they have departed. By strategic
use of the incomplete image he vivified the missing: absence of hearts, absence of towns, emptiness of prison cells.

The dominant characteristic of Eluard in his earliest
surrealist poetry was the love theme. In his later period,
love remained for him, as well as for Aragon and Breton,
an expression of the innermost recesses of human personality. A spontaneous physical and spiritual relationship with the loved one makes her the intermediary
between the creative sensibility of the poet and the sensations to be conjured from the earth. In her are reflected

the beauties of the material world and the impressions
of the poet. Love makes the senses keener and the imagination more acute, delivers the poet better than anything
else from the notions of time and space; love is at the
same time the center and the circumference of his universe: "world where without you I have nothing." [5] From
personal love to communion with all of humanity is a
natural step and one which inspired him to say, despite all the hatred about him: "I love for the sake of loving and I shall die of love." [6]

It is in *Poésie ininterrompue,* written immediately after
the termination of hostilities, that Eluard gave his
most complete expression of his parallel loves for his wife
and for humanity, and the ultimate relationship of these
feelings with the universe. With the surrealist's belief that
this world is all, and that there is enough here if only
we develop sufficient elasticity of insight, he proceeded
from the narrow perception of the blind of eye and of
heart to the apocalypse of the visionary. He draws upon
multiple perspectives as he and his loved one rise step by
step, widening the scope of their senses and exploring
their powers of divination. First the range of sight is
limited: walls, trees, rain; along with the physical barriers there is an isolationist aspect to the love enclosing
the two in a world of elemental needs. And this relationship has in the background the stolid contradictions
in universal man: his slow-moving barbarism, his stagnation, confusion of instincts, his blindness, his flashes of
insight:

L'homme aux lentes barbaries
L'homme comme un marais
L'homme à l'instinct brouillé
A la chair en exil
L'homme aux clartés de serre
Aux yeux fermés l'homme aux éclairs
L'homme mortel et divisé
Au front saignant d'espoir
L'homme en butte au passé
Et qui toujours regrette
Isolé quotidien
Dénué responsable

Then, he proceeds to a closer contact with the disorder of the world. The pace quickens, movement sets in, words like *new, open, light, awake, dawn, laughter* precipitate a succession of images with which love repossesses the world. His vision fluctuates between darkness and light, between reminiscences and foresight. Exterior calamities and the miracles of love struggle to mold to their respective dimensions the human habitat. Moral conviction of right and wrong results from his gradual cognizance of the real world, which he then molds to the dream. But these are not phantom dreams; they are the quintessence of sensuous experiences of the most unrestrained contact with the light and warmth of the world. The earthly dreams have love as their center:

Through you I go from light to light
From warmth to warmth
Through you I speak and you remain the center
Of all things like a sun consenting to my bliss

[Par toi je vais de la lumière à la lumière
De la chaleur à la chaleur
C'est par toi que je parle et tu restes au centre
De tout comme un soleil consentant au bonheur]

There is no juvenile cry of revolt or weary pessimism but virile struggle against the physical forces of evil with weapons that have no superhuman qualities. It is a step by step rejection of the past, a gradual enrichment of existence, an entrance into a four-dimensional world of freedom in which the words *infinite* and *immortal* are the treasured possessions of those who have learned to hope and be faithful to life on earth:

Everything is emptied and refilled
To the rhythm of the infinite

[Tout se vide et se remplit
Au rhythme de l'infini]

As they rise by degrees in the climate of love which thrives under "the sky's exploded screen," the images of earth are "reconquered" with greater and greater intensity, and their eyes open wider and wider upon a universe rife with miracles:

And midnight ripens fruit
And midday ripens moons

[Et minuit mûrit des fruits
Et midi mûrit des lunes]

Life is a limitless mirror where the eyes becoming immortal find the reflection of all things.

But the mirror was to break. Eluard suffered soon after the war the excruciating tragedy of losing his beloved wife, Nusch, in an accident. He and his friends did not think that he could survive the devastating blow nor bear the resulting solitude. Yet, his next volume, *Une Leçon de morale,* is a reiteration and a reinforcement of faith in the ability of a poet to transform the world and attain its inner unity. "Can one imagine earth and heaven divorced, can one think of a hand without fingers, a soul without a body, a dawn without light, a conscience without an aim" he asks in the preface to the volume. Therefore, though happiness is gone, he would consider it a "vice" to replace it with pessimism. Wavering between dejection (le Mal) and self-persuasion (le Bien) the poet triumphs over despair:

Like a miner who thinks of light
The light that rises in his heart

[Comme un mineur qui songe au jour
Le jour son coeur le fait monter]

He finds comfort in measuring his loss against humanity's eternity: "And if I lose—others will gain." He turns to the future as Apollinaire had before him:

Here comes tomorrow to reign today on earth

[Voici demain qui règne aujourd'hui sur la terre]

His rise out of grief has a cosmic rather than emotional character, the heart outspaces space and life conquers death:

The heart has so much space it defies the stars
It is like a wave that has no need to ebb
It is like a spring eternalizing flesh
The majesty of life that gives the lie to death

[Le coeur a tant d'espace qu'il défie les astres
Il est comme une vague qui n'a pas de fin
Il est comme une source éternisant la chair
La majesté de vivre désavoue la mort]

Though motivated by special circumstances, these post-war works of Aragon and Eluard give clear evidence of the aesthetic continuity of surrealism: the survival of the cult of the image and the resulting *rapprochement* of the subject and the object; a mystical approach to temporal events; free association of metaphors with a disregard for logical sequence; and a composite expression of physical and spiritual love. Their *post*-surrealism was an evolution rather than a change: increasing consciousness of the social message of the poet; and with this feeling there arose an increasing wish to communicate with a public, which implies a modification of their use of language.

In the April 1947 issue of *Europe,* in an article about the surrealist, Desnos, Aragon proclaimed that with the passing of surrealism would also pass the excessive liberty that the surrealists, including himself, had given to words; and he urged a return to the elementary language of common sense. He said that he had learned once more to call things by their right names. But one must be wary of accepting verbatim the self-analysis of a poet! Obscurity

was never a *sine qua non* of surrealism. It had been a reaction to the limitations that had been imposed on the
meaning of words, as we have noted previously, just as
free verse had been a protest against the abuse of the
alexandrine. If the immediate result of the revolt had
been complete loss of control of sense and form, it indicated only the swinging of the pendulum. The need
for discourse manifested by Aragon and Eluard was not
essentially a contradiction of former concepts of style;
from the first, surrealism had been seeking the elemental,
naked reality of words. What made surrealist poetry ob-
scure was not the misuse of words, but too succinct an association of ideas, too great a condensation of imagery,
coupled with extreme verbal concisions. In his preface to
En Etrange Pays dans mon pays lui-même Aragon had
pointed out that the secret of poetry for him was "to create
indestructible liaisons of words." His belief in the conjura-
tion of words is in the tradition of Baudelaire and of the
linguistic doctrines of the surrealists: that writing should
be a magical operation capable of producing enchantment. As long as for Aragon and Eluard the mating of
words, originality of verbal associations, hypnotic allitera-
tions remained a higher literary criterion than the expression of logical meaning, they never could actually achieve
the banality of the newspaper lingo that they decided to
emulate. During and after the war what they really elim-
inated from their style were eccentricities of language
and not its power of multiple implication. The change,
a somewhat forced one, did not fundamentally alter the
works written in the 1940's.

The change in language became drastic only when the political schism between Breton and his followers on the one hand, and Aragon and Eluard on the other, became categorical. As early as 1925 the surrealists had felt that their aesthetic ideals bore a subtle relation to social consciousness. To transform the world meant social as well as spiritual change. For a while, therefore, they had all identified this desire for a new social order with the communist revolution and made attempts at union with the communist organ, *Clarté.* Victor Crastre explained the "drama" of the attempted union in two issues of *Les Temps Modernes* in 1948: "The surrealists discovered that without social revolution there could not be a surrealist revolution." [7] He quoted Breton, himself, as writing in *Clarté:* "The isolation of the poet, the thinker, the artist from the masses, which is mutually harmful, is a result of the tactics of those who feel that they themselves stand to lose from this association. I want to believe that there does not exist a work of the intellect which is not conditioned by a real wish to improve the living conditions of the people." [8]

But Breton, as well as many of his colleagues and disciples, soon realized that their poetic image of "revolution" was in direct contradiction with the limited sense given the word by the communists. The surrealist orientation toward communism had been a philosophical one. The real object of their "torment" was "the human condition over and above the social condition of individuals." [9] But since they were concerned in enriching the life experience of humanity at large rather than in developing a few Nietzschean supermen, the social improvement seemed a prerequisite. In the 1920's interest in communism had been a "bravura" gesture on their part.[10] In the 1930's it had been based on sentimental adherence to Lenin's concepts, and a means of protest against France's foreign policies. The formal rift with communism came in 1935 following the cold reception that the surrealists received at the International Congress for the Defense of Culture, held in Moscow, when the majority of them, including Eluard signed the official manifesto severing all relations with the U.S.S.R.[11]

In a later statement, "Pour un art révolutionnaire indépendant," written in 1938,[12] André Breton further clarified his stand: although his concept of art was revolutionary he could no longer consider current communism as representative of that spirit. Moreover, the artist, who found it hard to accept any kind of authority, certainly could not bend to foreign directives. Eluard supported Breton's stand prior to World War II and it was not until 1943 when filled with the memories of comrades of the Resistance he returned to communist affiliations, which he maintained until his death in 1952.

Through all the surrealist polemics, Aragon maintained his original adherence to the Party, and even the Russian insults to surrealism did not affect his allegiance. He preferred to lose his former friends. But the penetration of the communist influence into his work was a gradual one. As we have seen in the poems of the war period and those collected soon after the war, his surrealism is tinged more with patriotic fervor than with communism. It is not until some years later that Aragon went as far as to declare that all his work as an artist had to be henceforth subjugated to the communist dream.

A collection of poems by Aragon, *Les Yeux et la mémoire,* and one by Eluard, *Les Sentiers et les routes de la poésie,* both appearing in 1954, show to what extent communism eventually overwhelmed surrealism in these two poets. In these volumes one can no longer discern any of the verbal technique we have noted in the earlier post-war works. Aragon's verse has the epic tone of Hugo; and Eluard's simplicity, which with the surrealist perspective had a ubiquitous elusiveness, becomes in these posthumously published poems limpingly prosaic and monotonously evangelical in cadence.

It is amazing how in adopting the partisan line, two poets of such differing personality sound alike. The surrealist cult of the future, exemplified often in the prophetic dream or in the visionary image, is appropriated, narrowed down in meaning, and identified with the communist dream of a future utopia. Eluard dreams of a "paradise on earth" in which it would be the poet's function to prove himself "more useful than any other citizen of the tribe." [13] Aragon echoes the same ideology as he declares that every word he utters from now on will belong to tomorrow: "all dream of the future is a dream to live." To live in a world happy as the song of a turtledove! "Where the happiness of all is the happiness of each," such is his "new humanity." Even death is not really death to those who are harnessed to the "great dream" which says Aragon cannot fail, for they have

shaken off the security of the kind of life that is greedily
limited to itself:

Mourir n'est plus mourir à ceux-là qui s'attellent
Au grand rêve de tous qui ne peut avorter
Ils sont hommes d'avoir secoué la tutelle
D'une vie à soi seul chichement limitée
Et le héros d'hier lui donnant sa mesure
Chaque jour plus nombreuse à l'assaut de l'azur
C'est la nouvelle humanité.[14]

The rationalizing character of this latter-day verse of
Aragon and Eluard negatively demonstrates, to what extent the linguistic technique had been an integral part
of the surrealist turn of mind; the acceptance of a mystical reality within the orbit of earthly existence. When
the mysticism vanished the language vanished with it.
War and the occupation of France had not destroyed in
Aragon's and Eluard's poetry this metaphysical vision;
but what the war could not do, the cold war and its in-
doctrination did. They lost their surrealist art only when
they compromised and, giving up the search for the absolute, agreed to settle for merely a social transformation
of the earth.

Strangely, the year 1959 offers an epilogue to Aragon's
post-surrealism. The man who, for the last decade allegedly had eyes only for the future has, it now appears,
for three years been very much engrossed with the past:
the year 1815, vividly, poetically restored in his novel, *La
Semaine sainte,* which has won him tremendous acclaim
and returned him, as it were, to the family of French

literary men from whom his party had separated him for thirty-two years.

In the midst of this warm reception he has found it in his heart to recall his surrealist past. In an article about a young novelist, Philippe Sollers, he reminisces about his own youth, contrasting the bonds of fraternity among the surrealists with the loneliness and isolation of young writers today. At this late date he declares that he has never ceased to be a surrealist and that he has never held any grudge against André Breton, whom he considers one of the truly great writers of France.

"Life separated us, set us one against the other . . . All the newcomers and the old friends of my youth. They will never be able to prevent my considering them as my own. Even with political abysses between us, which I am not ready to bridge. . . . I have always defended the skies of my youth." [15]

Some have wanted to see in these recent statements a proof of a change of heart in Aragon. It may be so, although Aragon insists that only as a communist could he have written *La Semaine sainte*. However, the problem of his present or future political affiliations are not really significant for this study. What cannot be changed is that he, along with his friend Eluard, were part of the spiritual adventure called surrealism, and exemplified in dramatic fashion its evolution from early rebellion to optimistic faith in the powers of the human imagination to transform the world, fortified by a growing moral awareness of that world. If in a later stage the dream was reduced to political terms, the previous work has an existence independent of its author, and as the author cannot forget his former friends, his works cannot deny their surrealist imprint.

N O T E S

1. Aragon, *Le Paysan de Paris*, Gallimard, 1926, p. 236.

2. *Ibid.*, p. 81.

3. Aragon, *Cantique à Elsa*, "Ce que dit Elsa."

4. Eluard, *Les Dessous d'une vie*, p. 17. First introduced in this work the image is used frequently elsewhere.

5. Eluard, *Le Livre ouvert*, "Je veux qu'elle soit reine," p. 52.

6. Eluard, *Poésie ininterrompue*, Gallimard, 1946, p. 17.

7. Victor Crastre, "Le drame du surréalisme," *Les Temps Modernes*, July 1948, p. 60.

8. *Ibid.*, August, 1948, p. 305.

9. Breton, *Entretiens*, Gallimard, 1952, p. 124.

10. See "La Claire Tour," *La Clé des champs:* "around 1925 only the IIIrd International seemed to furnish the means of transforming the world," p. 273.

11. In *Entretiens* Breton goes over the incidents that led to the rift. Ilya Ehrenbourg had written a book, *Seen by a writer from U.S.S.R.* in which he had insulted the surrealists by treating them as loafers and suggesting that they had squandered their wives' dowries. Meeting him one day on a street in Paris on the eve of the Congress, Breton had given in to the impulse of slapping Ehrenbourg in the face. As a result Breton was not permitted to give his scheduled speech at the Congress. All the pleadings of his colleagues were of no avail. This refusal disturbed René Crevel to such an extent that he committed suicide as an act of protest on the eve of the meeting. Finally, Eluard was allowed to read Breton's statement but he was rudely interrupted in the middle of it and was not allowed to finish. After that, Breton would never

again have anything to do with the U.S.S.R. and called it a land of tyranny.

12. This manifesto was signed by Breton and Diego Rivera, written in Mexico. Breton confesses in *Entretiens* that his collaborator was really Trotsky.

13. Eluard, *Les Sentiers et les routes de la poésie,* Gallimard, 1954, p. 126.

14. Aragon, *Les Yeux et la mémoire,* Gallimard, 1954, p. 101.

15. Aragon, *Les Lettres Françaises,* Nov. 1958.

◐

to transform the world

While the poetry of Aragon and Eluard suffered devia-
tions and then complete transformation after World War
II, surrealism itself as a literary unit disintegrated when
its members were dispersed to the four corners of the
earth. After the war, the surrealist "evidence," originally
only to be found in the works of individual poets or demonstrated in reviews such as *Les Quatre Vents* or *Medium,*
has established its imprint on poetic language and as a phi-

losophy of life. Thereafter, surrealist activities no longer could be concerted, organized gestures or the demonstration of doctrines. But the untiring and uncompromising character of André Breton has continued to serve as a stimulation to literary and artistic work which aspires to expand the field of human imagination.

Although Breton left France during the war and shrank from the idea of writing circumstantial verse, the war brought him great personal bereavement, the effects of which he could not exclude from his poetry despite his distance from the mêlée. Whereas Aragon wished his poetry "to read like a newspaper," as he explained in his *Chronique du Bel Canto,* Breton tried to keep the specifically circumstantial aspects of the world cataclysm out of his work. But anyone who saw Breton in those war years realized how impossible it would have been for him to separate his grief over Europe's disaster from his purely literary activities. Besides, was literature ever *pure* for André Breton? Perhaps more than anyone since Baudelaire, he has accepted writing as an integral part of his life experience.

This was a period of great travels for Breton in the Western Hemisphere, whose grandiose landscapes supplied him with a constant stimulus for the type of imagery that could counterbalance the message-compulsion created in him by the troubled times.

Les Etats Généraux (1943) contained a social message, preached tolerance, the basic oneness of the world. He envisaged a people rising to the sense of interdependence, realizing the wealth of human power that could be gen-

erated from the free intermingling of the genius of all
races of the world, and first of all turning to the black
and red races: "Because they have been for a long time
the most abused." However, the message is illuminated
by Breton's marvelous power over language, his constant
discovery of lost words and their hypnotic uses which
transform the world more than do his twentieth-century
sociological ideas!

Breton's vein of imagery is inexhaustible and would
grant total escape from the miseries of the world if he
so desired—and it actually does so in some of his love
poems. But Breton refuses to be transported by the image.
Rather, he puts it to work in dramatizing the need to
change the world.

Breton's notion of the absolute is altered by the war
years as was that of Aragon and Eluard. His preoccupation shifts from the spiritual and sensual to the moral
field, where his vision, he says, will hold an unlimited
empire:

La vision nocturne a été quelque chose il s'agit
Maintenant de l'étendre du physique au moral
Où son empire sera sans limite.

The transformation of the world must be sparked by an
improvement in the moral caliber of man. Mallarmé's
"coup de dés" has its counterpart in Breton's flipping of
the coin to see which way the world will go. "Heads"
would signal emptiness, but it falls on "tails," which represents the unconscious yet irresistible bent toward the better:

Pile ou face face la pièce nue libre de toute effigie
    de tout millésime
Pile
La pente insensible et pourtant irresistible vers le mieux

But unlike Aragon and Eluard, he keeps free of political
involvements. Breton's moral concern is not channeled toward any present social system. Instead, he salutes the
nineteenth-century philosopher Fourier and calls upon
him as a humanitarian and a visionary to cast his light
upon the drab ideas and aspirations of our time:

Fourier tranchant sur la grisaille des idées et des aspirations
    d'aujourd'hui ta lumière.

He wrote this *Ode to Fourier*, which he considers one of
his principal post-war writings, while on a journey through
the American Far West. The Petrified Forest seemed to
him symbolic of the condition of the world and its need
for stimulation.

Je te salue de la Forêt Pétrifiée de la culture humaine
Où plus rien n'est debout
Mais où rodent de grandes lueurs tournoyantes
Qui appellent la délivrance du feuillage et de l'oiseau
De tes doigts part la sève des arbres en fleurs

Although he expresses discouragement at such moments, the tone that generally permeates his post-war
writing is not one of pessimism. In *Entretiens* (1952) when
he was asked by the interviewer if he agreed with Camus
that the modern Sisyphus must roll his stone and try to
enjoy life within the limits of his inescapable chore, Bre-

ton's answer was characteristic of the vigorous optimism
that has consistently accompanied him through both his
sublime and catastrophic moments. Why accept as a final
and irrevocable punishment what can be annulled! Why
put greater confidence in the durability of the rock than
in man's potential power to destroy it and thereby overcome the absurdity of the task?

"One day or another it will break, abolishing as if by
enchantment the mountain and its punishment." [1]

Nowhere in Breton's writings is the vitality of surrealism better revealed nor the stature of its author. Breton's
reaction to the myth of Sisyphus is in a sense a protest
against the tendency of the humanistic philosophies of the
West since the time of Pascal to rationalize the miseries of
the human condition by vesting it with an illusion of
dignity.

Few have had in our time as close and as constant an
awareness of the tragic reality of human existence as
Breton who identifies the essential tragedy of man not
with his social or moral condition but with "the flagrant
disproportion between the breadth of man's aspirations
and the individual limits of his life." [2] Yet this incon-
gruity between the span of life and the scope of human
desire has never discouraged Breton. Is he naïve, then?
On the contrary it is his extreme sophistication that raises
him above dejection and gives him not a grim but a gallant optimism. For the optimism is based on the assump-
tion that existence is not final, nor static, nor limited, but
subject to change, to fortuitous but predictable modification. Therefore, whatever is tragic is transitory, relative,

and not an obstacle in man's progress toward the absolute.

When asked if he had any regrets about his life or work, Breton answered that his life had been lived exactly according to his dream of life. Although as much as any priest André Breton has had to keep the vow of poverty, although he has lived to see lesser writers than himself win greater public acclaim, he has shown no regrets. In maintaining an uncompromising attitude toward the principles of surrealism, he has been willing to accept the sometimes unhappy consequences: the quarrels, and the solitudes, and the disconcerting reality of not being able to earn a living like his more pliable colleagues. He has exemplified not the pure but the *total* poet, clarifying to a greater degree than anyone in our time, what the position of a poet can be in society: not to seek to please and be admired, but to know and to communicate knowledge.

Among those who passed through the surrealist experience, two poets have won recognition in the post-war years both in France and abroad: René Char and Antonin Artaud, one for the positive values of his poetry which has crystallized many of the surrealist concepts, the other for the surrealist life which he has allegedly lived and the negative character of his behavior which has struck a sympathetic note in the post-war younger generation.

René Char, half a generation younger than André Breton, appears to carry on the tradition of surrealism better than anyone else, although he has supposedly gone through and beyond surrealism. Like Breton, simply and completely a poet, he has faced up to "this rebellious and solitary world of contradictions" as he terms it in *Le Poème pulvérisé,* and has decided that it is impossible to live without having the image of the unknown ever before one's eyes. His universe, built as Breton's, upon a structure of metaphysical metaphors, is a place of discovery, where even "the harvest of the abyss" is a possibility. The poet's task in this life, whose limits he calls "immense" is to "extract from things the illusion they produce to preserve themselves from us" and, on the other hand, to let them keep that part which they would willingly yield to us. "The pulverized poem" represents this effort to remove the trappings of reality and to uncover what nature begrudges man.

"Il y aura toujours une goutte d'eau pour durer plus que le soleil sans que l'ascendant du soleil soit ébranlé." His concept of poetry, like Breton's is one of salutary foresight, intended to enhance human qualities.

Writing with a brilliance and a freshness unmarred by any allegiance or engagement to anything but the dictates of his destiny as poet, Char has gained a quiet but well-anchored fame.

Antonin Artaud has been the other side of the coin, personifying not the art but the legend of the surrealist. He is the one, says Breton, who went right through the mirror. Unbalanced, later totally deranged, he was committed for a number of years to a mental hospital. Eventually he managed to get out only to end his tormented existence in suicide.

This dark angel of surrealism, representing the initial

pessimism and revolt of the group, rather than its later manifestation of constructive poetic vision, has had a special appeal for the "angry" or "beat" avant-garde. In his notorious letter from Rodez (the hospital) he demonstrated the rebellious, impudent disgust of the young generation of 1920:

"People are stupid. Literature empty. There is nothing more and nobody left, the soul is insane, there is no more love, nor even any hatred left, all the bodies satiated, consciences resigned. There is not even any anxiety left, which has vanished into the emptiness of bones." [3]

While most of the members of the surrealist group abandoned this obvious sort of criticism of the state of contemporary society, Artaud never grew out of it, never went beyond the feeling of contempt for the absurdity of the world. The present cult of the absurd, reminiscent of the Dada atmosphere of the first post-war period, has found a symbol in the tormented Artaud. It would be unfortunate if Artaud's personal mishaps were to be confused with the surrealist adventure.

Today the surrealist élan may seem out of place in a literary atmosphere dominated on the one hand by the anguish of sober-faced existentialists, and on the other by the dark, sordid humour of a group of dazzling non-French writers who are living in Paris, writing in French and seeming to revive the spirit of the Dada era. For a time surrealism may become merely an undercurrent, instead of flowing full-stream into the literary consciousness. Literary graftings such as Beckett's and Ionesco's produce in general late blossoms—which may explain the flowering of a new dadaism thirty years late. But the last flower, though often more brilliant than the early one, proves also more ephemeral. This latter-day dadaism translates only the apparent despair of our epoch. For, although the ills of the human condition and the man-willed ones of war are still glaringly with us, there is an inner dynamism in these times that makes pseudo-dadaism seem myopic, and the surrealist outlook more truly representative of the spirit of our age with its unrelenting, ever accelerating drive for enterprise and exploration. Belief in the inner resources of man, which might, if cultivated, transform the world, is a continuation of the prescience of Guillaume Apollinaire, who in the midst of the last world catastrophe foresaw for humanity much vaster domains in which to exercise his liberty. It is an optimism comparable with "voyance," it is the point beyond nihilism, which is perhaps the realization of the futility of nihilism. And "tremors" greater than those that crossed Lautréamont's intellectual horizon indicate today that the dream carries reality in its tracks.

N O T E S

1. Breton, *Entretiens,* p. 248.

2. *Ibid.,* p. 266.

3. Antonin Artaud, "Lettre de Rodez," *L'Evidence surréaliste,* in *Les Quatre Vents,* no. 4, p. 185.

◖

the world transformed

Today surrealism does not need to prove the authenticity of its position, for science challenging man's utmost imaginative resources has followed a parallel path of inquiry and is itself proving the poet's hypothesis with more tangible evidence.

Early in the twentieth century Einstein unraveled the imprecisions of time and space; the progress of nuclear physics in the past twenty-five years has shaken the concept of chronology. Science has also proved that the principles of causality, which for centuries had made determinism an essential axiom of materialism, are no longer tenable; for the caprices of the physical world have been found to be governed by the unpredictable rate and timing of atomic radiation. Rather, it is chance —the "divine hazard" of the surrealists—and theories of probability that are needed to gauge the dynamism of matter. Statistical calculation rather than rational theorems serve to approximate—not measure exactly—time, space, chronology, and the infinite variations of an ever incomplete and therefore limitless universe. It is Mallarmé's "coup de dés" which is governing our existence and our knowledge of it. In rejecting the principle of causality the scientist with all his tools of reasoning confirms the surrealists' intuition that there can be a nondeterminist understanding of reality.

In a significant article, "The Image of Nature according to Contemporary Physics," [1] the renowned German scientist, Werner Heisenberg, suggests that developments in modern atomic physics must have repercussions in the field of philosophy. His description of the relation between objective reality and man's intervention in it seems to have been taken directly from the pages of surrealist aesthetics.

First, according to Heisenberg, there was nature marked by God. Then man learned to envisage nature objectively, giving a somewhat simplified image of the universe. But the intervention of man's technical faculties in the observation of nature has resulted in abolishing the concept of an independent, static image. Man with his new methods and tools of observation has actually transformed "on a large scale" the world that serves as his environment, and he has marked it with the human seal. As a result the line between the subject and the object is vanishing.

"The knowledge of atoms and their movements 'on their own', i.e. independently of our experimental observation is no longer the purpose of research: we find ourselves from the start in the midst of a dialogue between nature and man, in which science plays only a partial role, so that the division between subject and object, of inner and outer world, in body and soul can no longer be applied and raises difficulties."

The scientist can no longer contemplate and investigate nature objectively but submits it to human questioning and ever links it to the destiny of man. Thus by his method he transforms the object and can no longer separate himself from the purpose of his quest.

These are not verbalizations of a poet but the affirmations of a scientist, revealing inadvertently but dramatically the actuality of surrealism, of Breton's vision of the crisis of the object, and of Max Ernst's prophecy of the more general crisis of conscience that might rise out of it. Indeed, will the joint utilization of the new techniques of the artist and of the scientist establish in our time a new relationship between man and the universe?

Artists have always first presented their visions, and the scientists have then provided substance for these conjectures of the imagination. The surrealists on their road to the absolute are in search of new myths to symbolize the new visions. The myth of Sisyphus is obsolete, even with modern variations, for it is the artistic symbol of a social reality that has been long extinct. It is no longer in the nature of man to roll stones, but to cut them, not to struggle up mountains but to blast passages through them, as centuries of his history can attest. It is one thing to appreciate Greek symbols for their beauty, for the authenticity of their meaning in their time, but to appropriate them and to try to adapt them to the needs of an entirely different age, seems to show lack of imagination as well as a lack of a sense of historical truth. The myth of Sisyphus (as well as that of Icarus) is incompatible with the astronauts' mission of conquest. The premises for the transformation of man's social condition have already been laid, and if physical slavery has not yet been totally banished from the world, release from it has been proved possible, therefore it can no longer be considered an inevitable part of the human condition. Philosophies and literatures, then, which use the physical bondage of man as a point of departure are laboring with an old-time model. Man has already found a greater diversity and flexibility in the employment of his time on earth. He has freedom of movement in an ever widening orbit. His actions are self-willed even if he often appears to act by rote. In many parts of the world he has earned—often paying for it dearly—a certain freedom of thought. But it is a limited thing, this freedom to think, the freedom to dream, unless the mind strives forever to widen its comprehension, to multiply the possibilities of its perception! Perhaps the aspiration to immortality, heretofore manifested in the effort to increase the life span, would find more satisfaction in intensifying the mind's speculative forces. For reality will be as narrow or as vast as man's power to envisage it. It is this spiritual progress of man, "a greater emancipation of the mind," as Breton calls it, which is the chief concern of the future, and it is up to the artist to provide new myths to dramatize it.

Lautréamont's appeal today is due to the fact that his anguish over the biological condition of man took the larger proportions of a spiritual combat. Likewise, Apollinaire's notion of human progress was based on the desire for man to attain spiritual heights by becoming "more pure, more live, more learned." So too, the timeliness of surrealism lies in its emphasis on the need to enlarge the orbit of the human intellect.

The endeavors of the scientist and the artist in this field seem to be closely linked. With the unraveling of cosmic mysteries, the keys of nature may, as Breton hopes, be at last within man's reach. In such an atmosphere of expectancy, literature needs more than ever before the vitality of those whose objective it is to enhance the forces of imagination. Instead, current fiction supplies us with an ever lengthening gallery of non-heroic characters, asphyxiating in their limited worlds from which they seek no exit. If the novel-genre persists in developing along lines so incongruous to these times, surrealism's dynamic adventure is, by contrast, a signal to the poet to maintain the heroic role in literature.

N O T E S

1. Werner Heisenberg, "La Nature selon la physique contemporaine," *La Nouvelle Revue Française,* jan.-fev. 1959.

epilogue

Poetry has proved to be the frailest of the Muses, yet like the delicate weed of the fable it bends but does not break in the powerful currents of changing literary *genres*. The vitality that surrealism has injected into the ailing but long-lived invalid, is being recognized more and more by French poets and critics, by those who themselves did not share in the literary revolution that surrealism unleashed in the 1920's. Many writers in other parts of the world, trying to adapt other languages to the perspectives of today, are appreciating and emulating the changes in the use of language that the French surrealists achieved, and which transformed the most regulated, grammatically precise language, into the most liberated, winged accomplice of literary imagination. Consciously or unconsciously the style of many a formal French Academician has been affected by the work of these linguistic pioneers. The clichés of analogy which still clutter so much of the poetry of other languages seem to have been radically removed from the French literary language. It is an example that the literatures of other countries, some quickly, others belatedly, have been following. The study of the increasing influence of surrealism on non-French literatures will deserve to be the object of many a future investigation by literary historians.

The ripples of the movement are even now lapping our shores. Significantly, it is the young writer in America, and not the contemporaries of André Breton or even of René Char who are receptive to the repercussions of surrealism. More than any other readers I have had them in mind in writing of the French poets' "Road to the Absolute."

As I add these concluding lines I realize that I may have seemed at times belligerent toward symbolists and traditional writers. The successful need no praise. The public richly rewards obvious merits without the assistance of the critic. In assuming the role of devil's advocate I am not insensible to the beauties of symbolist poetry, nor oblivious to the polish of the modern novel.

I also realize that there are novelists and dramatists today who are endeavoring to break the barriers of the traditions of those *genres*. Novelists such as Alain Robbe-Grillet and Maurice Butor have seized with new eyes the world of objects that surround contemplative man, and like their predecessors the poets of the previous generation, they are trying to establish new relationships between the concrete world and the writer's introspections. The great difference which Hegel signalized between romanticism and the modern spirit, is being demonstrated in the novel today by those who cease to absorb within their subconscious world the objective reality which they encounter, but instead attempt to project the human web into the orbit of non-subjective existence. On the other hand, the dramatist has been utilizing the dark humor of the surrealist heritage in creating the drama of illogical reality.

It remains to be seen if these technical feats are to be endowed with the artistic idealism which marked the surrealist credo. For it was this faith in the potential powers of the human mind over both the subjective world and the world of concrete reality which made of surrealism a worthy successor to the classical ideal.

index

of authors and artists

◑

APOLLINAIRE, Guillaume, *12-13,* 14, 48, *50-69,* 78, 116, 121, 122, 136, 141n, 142, 178, 196, 201.

APOLLINAIRE, Jacqueline (Madame) 68.

ARAGON, Louis, *16,* 37n, 47, 57, 67, 87, 93, 105, 106, 113, 114, 118, 119, 133, 135, 140n, 141n, 147, 161, *165-187,* 188, 189, 190, 191.

ACHIM VON ARNIM, 103.

ARTAUD, Antonin, *193-6.*

BAUDELAIRE, Charles, 4, *6, 7,* 8, 18n, 21, 82, 119, 140, 144, 167, 180, 189.

BECKETT, Samuel, 195.

BLAKE, William, 6, 18n.

BLANCHOT, Maurice, 37n.

BENDA, Julien, 103.

BRETON, André, 5, 15, 16, 18, 18n, 19n, 21, 22, 31, 37n, 39, 41, 45, 47, 67, 87, *91-111,* 112, 113, 114, 115, 116, 117, 118, *120-130,* 138-39, 140n, 141n, 142, 143, 144, 145, 147, 149, 154, 158, 161n, 166, 174, *181-182,* 185, *189-93,* 194, 199, 201.

BRAQUE, George, 59, 143.

BRAUNER, Victor, 153.

BRUN, Jean, 120, 140n.

CAILLOIS, Roger, 37n.

CAMUS, Albert, 37n, 191.

CHAGALL, Marc, 155.

CHAR, René, 67, 120, 127, *193-6.*

CHASSE, Charles, 19n.

CHIRICO, Giorgio de, 83, *143, 144,* 145, 151, 152.

CLAUDEL, Paul, 70, 166.

COMTE, Auguste, 23.

CRASTRE, Victor, 181, 186.

CREVEL, René, 14, 15, 19n, 106, 108, 109, 110, 122, *186n.*

DALI, Salvador, 96, 98, 122, 145, 149, 150, 151, 152, 153, 155, *156,* 160.

DUCASSE, Isidore, 20, 22, 37; see also Comte de Lautréamont.

DARWIN, Charles, 24, 25, 26, 27, 32, 37n.

DESNOS, Robert, 95, 110n, 134, 141n, 179.

DU BELLAY, Joachim, 136.

DUCHAMP, Marcel, 151.

EHRENBOURG, Ilya, 186.

EINSTEIN, Albert, 197.

ELIOT, T. S., 10.

ELUARD, Paul, 21, 41, 67, 87, 93, 97, 98, 106, 111n, 113, 114, 115, 120, 124, 126, 130-133, 134, 143, 152, 161n, *165-187*, 188, 190, 191.
ENGELS, Paul, 104.
ERNST, Max, 103, 122, 145, 150, 151, *154*, 155, 160, 161n, 199.

FEUERBACH, Anselme, 103.
FOURIER, Charles, 191.
FRAIS-WITTMAN, 110n.
FRANCE, Anatole, 113.
FREUD, Sigmund, 14, 15, 91, 96, 97, *99-102, 108, 109,* 111n.

GAUTIER, Théophile, fils, 103.
GIACOMETTI, Alberto, 145, 157.
GANZO, Robert, 42, 50n.
GIDE, André, 45.
GOETHE, 100.
GOMEZ DE LA SERNA, Ramón, 67.
GRACQ, Julien, 37n.

HAUPTMANN, Gerhardt, 4.
HEGEL, 45, *91, 94, 103-110,* 111n.
HEISENBERG, Werner, 198, 202n.
HITLER, Adolph, 104.
HUGO, Victor, 10, 27, 183.
HUYSMANS, J. K., 4.

IONESCO, 195.

JACOB, Max, 60.

KAFKA, Franz, 35.
KANT, Emmanuel, 103.
KIERGEGAARD, Soeren, 93.

LANGEL, Auguste, 24.
LAUTRÉAMONT, Comte de, 6, 8, *20-38,* 143, 154, 196, 201; see also Isidore Ducasse.
LENIN, V., 104, 105.
LEE, Gerald Stanley, 60, 69n.
LEIRIS, Michel, 117, 118, *125,* 140n.
LITTRÉ, Emile, 19n.
LOUIS-BRÉON, 54.

MAETERLINCK, Maurice, 12, 79.
MAGRITTE, René, 21, 157.
MALLARMÉ, Stéphane, 5, 6, *9-12,* 14, 16, 19n, 81, 115, 190, 198.
MARINETTI, F. T., 58.
MAURRAS, Charles, 166.
MARX, Karl, 103.
MEZEI, Arpad, 118, 140n.
MIRÓ, Joan, 151, 157.

NADEAU, Maurice, 111n.
NERVAL, Gérard de, 104.
NIETZSCHE, Frederic, 93.
NOUGÉ, Paul, *148, 149.*

ORTEGA Y GASSET, José, 59.

PASCAL, Blaise, 68.
PÉGUY, Charles, 166.
PÉRET, Benjamin, 21, 126.
PICABIA, Francis, 59.

PICASSO, Pablo, 59, *143, 144,* 150, *151,* 152, 161n.

POE, Edgar Allan, 133.

QUATREFOGES, A. de, 24.

RAPHAEL, 161.

RAY, Man, 156.

RENAN, Ernest, 24, 37n.

REVERDY, Pierre, 60, 69n, *70-88,* 121, 147, 154.

RIMBAUD, Arthur, 5, 6, *8, 9, 10,* 20, 21, 42, 44, 140, 145, 167.

RIVERA, Diego, 187n.

RENÉVILLE, Rolland de, 42.

ROUSSEAU, Henri (Le Douanier) 59.

ROY, Claude, 166.

ROYER, Clémence, 25, 32, 37n.

SAINT-POL-ROUX, 12, *39-49,* 60, 78, 98, 139, 143, 144, 154, 166.

SHAPIRO, Karl, 19n.

SHELLEY, Percy, 113.

SOLLERS, Philippe, 185.

SOUPAULT, Philippe, 21, 37n, 65, 67, 69n.

TANGUY, Yves, 101, *158-161.*

THINION, André, 104, 105, 111n.

TROTSKY, Leon, 187n.

TZARA, Tristan, 96, 98, 105, 111n, 113, 114, 125.

VALÉRY, Paul, 70.

VERLAINE, Paul, 9, 115.

VILLIERS de l'ISLE-ADAM, 7, 10.

DATE DUE

DEC 16 '64			
JAN 4 '65			
GAYLORD			PRINTED IN U.S.A.